Harvard
Business
Review

ON
STRATEGIES
FOR
GROWTH

THE HARVARD BUSINESS REVIEW PAPERBACK SERIES

The series is designed to bring today's managers and professionals the fundamental information they need to stay competitive in a fast-moving world. From the preeminent thinkers whose work has defined an entire field to the rising stars who will redefine the way we think about business, here are the leading minds and landmark ideas that have established the *Harvard Business Review* as required reading for ambitious businesspeople in organizations around the globe.

Other books in the series:

Harvard Business Review on Change

Harvard Business Review on Knowledge Management

Harvard Business Review on Leadership

Harvard Business Review on Measuring Corporate Performance

Harvard Business Review

ON

STRATEGIES

FOR

GROWTH

A HARVARD BUSINESS REVIEW PAPERBACK

The *Harvard Business Review* articles in this collection are available as individual reprints. Discounts apply to quantity purchases. For information and ordering please contact Customer
Service, Harvard Business School Publishing, Boston, MA 02163.
Telephone: (617) 783-7500 or (800) 988-0886, 8 A.M. to 6 P.M.
Eastern Time, Monday through Friday. Fax: (617) 783-7555, 24
hours a day. E-mail: custserv@hbsp.harvard.edu.

Library of Congress Catalog Card Number
99-160363

*The paper used in this publication meets the requirements of the
American National Standard for Permanence of Paper for Printed
Library Materials Z39.49-1984.*

Contents

Harvard Business Review

ON

STRATEGIES

FOR

GROWTH

Breaking Compromises, Breakaway Growth

GEORGE STALK, JR.,

DAVID K. PECAUT, AND

BENJAMIN BURNETT

Executive Summary

MANY COMPANIES TODAY are searching for growth. But how and where should they look? Breaking compromises can be a powerful organizing principle. Even in the most mature businesses, compromise breakers have emerged from the pack to achieve breakaway growth—far outpacing the rest of their industry. Examples include Chrysler Corporation, Contadina, CarMax, and the Charles Schwab Corporation.

Compromises are concessions customers are forced to make. Unlike trade-offs, which are the legitimate choices customers make between different product or service offerings, compromises are imposed. For instance, in choosing a hotel, a customer can *trade off* luxury for economy. But the entire hotel industry makes customers *compromise* by not permitting early check-in.

Trade-offs are very visible, but most compromises are hidden.

Compromises mean it's the industry's way or no way. Often, customers assume the industry must be right; they accept compromises as the way the business works. That is why traditional market research rarely uncovers compromise-breaking opportunities.

The authors propose a number of alternative approaches to finding the compromises hidden in any business. One approach is to look for the compensatory behaviors customers engage in because using the product or service as intended would not fully meet their needs. Other approaches include paying attention to performance anomalies and looking for diseconomies in the industry's value chain. If managers think like customers, the authors say, they will be able to find and exploit compromises for faster growth and improved profitability.

W HEN IS A MATURE, SLOW-GROWTH BUSINESS not a mature business? How do rapidly growing companies emerge from stagnant, dead-in-the-water industries? The station-wagon segment of the North American auto market was dying when, in 1984, Chrysler Corporation introduced the minivan. Over the next ten years, minivan sales grew eight times faster than did the industry overall. For the last 15 years, the do-it-yourself home-improvement business as a whole has grown barely 5% per year while Home Depot has racked up 20% growth. Over capacity and flat demand plague the airline industry, but that hasn't kept Southwest Airlines Company from growing seven times faster than the industry average over the past decade.

What senior managers at Chrysler, Home Depot, and Southwest have in common is the wisdom, curiosity, and perseverance to explore the compromises their industries were forcing customers to endure. And each acted on the insight that breaking those compromises would release enormous trapped value—enough to stimulate major sales and profit growth. In fact, the concept of breaking compromises is one of the most powerful organizing principles we have seen for companies that wish to achieve breakaway growth. (See the graphs in "Breakaway Growth: Compromise Breakers Have Outperformed Their Industries.")

Compromises are not trade-offs. Trade-offs are the legitimate choices customers make among different product or service offerings. Trade-offs typically come from fundamental differences in cost structures that are usually reflected in prices. With products, the trade-offs often arise from differences in design or in the cost of materials. With textiles, *Compromises occur when* for example, there is a *an industry imposes its own* trade-off between price *operating practices or* and quality because bet-*constraints on customers.* ter fabrics tend to have higher thread counts. In service, trade-offs are common because delivering greater convenience or customization often entails higher cost. Thus taxi service costs more than bus service, and a meal delivered by room service costs more than the same meal ordered in the hotel restaurant.

A compromise, in contrast, is a concession demanded of consumers by all or most service or product providers. Whereas trade-offs let customers choose

Breakaway Growth: Compromise Breakers Have Outperformed Their Industries

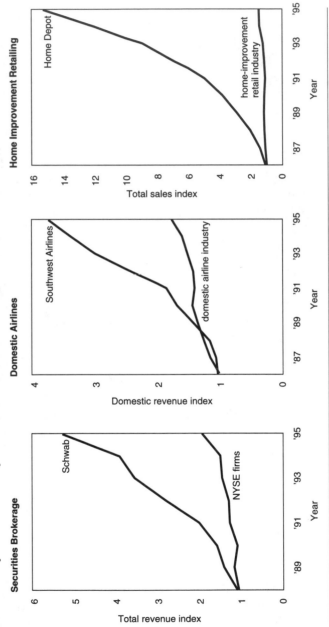

Securities Brokerage

Total revenue index — Schwab, NYSE firms — Year '89 '91 '93 '95

Domestic Airlines

Domestic revenue index — Southwest Airlines, domestic airline industry — Year '87 '89 '91 '93 '95

Home Improvement Retailing

Total sales index — Home Depot, home-improvement retail industry — Year '87 '89 '91 '93 '95

Source: The Boston Consulting Group.

their preference among alternatives, compromises offer no choice. Trade-offs allow different offerings to appeal to different segments; compromises benefit no particular segment. Trade-offs are very visible; most compromises are hidden.

In picking a hotel room, for instance, a customer can *trade off* luxury for economy by choosing between a Ritz-Carlton and a Best Western. But the hotel industry forces customers to *compromise* by not permitting check-in before 4 P.M. Similarly, until recently, most auto dealers forced a compromise on customers by not offering weekend repair and maintenance services. There is no law of nature that says that cars can't get fixed on weekends or that hotel rooms can't be ready before late afternoon. Compromises occur when an industry imposes its own operating practices or constraints on customers, leaving them no choice. It's the industry's way or no way. And often customers accept compromises as the way the business works.

Henry Ford's famous car in any color—as long as it's black—is one type of compromise. Such a compromise denies customers the selection they want. Or customers are forced to wait. Today's car buyer can custom-order virtually any car if the selection on the dealer's lot is inadequate, but the industry will make customers wait six to eight weeks for delivery. In other situations, customers may be forced to use a high-cost service or to pay a premium to get the quality they want. Because the family washing machine can't safely handle all fabrics, customers have to spend extra time and money on dry cleaning. The compromise often becomes visible when customers have to modify their behavior to use a company's product or service. Until recently, dishwashers did a satisfactory job of washing the dishes, but they made enough noise to wake the dead. Their owners had to arrange a time when they were out of hearing range to wash the dishes.

Compromises creep into businesses in various ways. Some, like hotel check-in times, are imposed by standard operating practices that no one questions. Others stem from conscious decisions that may make marginal economic sense—as long as customers adjust their behavior. For example, it may make sense for a supplier to deliver only once a week, but doing so forces customers to hold inventory between deliveries. The most important compromises, however, are forced on customers simply because companies have lost touch with those customers' needs. Finding and breaking those compromises can unleash new demand and create breakaway growth.

The Great Pasta Compromise

Contadina, an operating unit of Nestlé, has created a high-growth business by breaking the compromises imposed on consumers of pasta. Contadina's fresh pasta product is sold in supermarkets, cooks in minutes in boiling water, and comes in many varieties, including ravioli and tortellini.

Before Contadina's innovation, consumers faced one trade-off and a multitude of compromises in their quest to eat pasta. The trade-off was between eating pasta at home—where someone has to make it—and eating out at a restaurant. Pasta at home is less expensive. The restaurant has more variety and means less work, but it costs more.

The great pasta compromise begins after the decision to stay home and make it yourself. Homemade pasta is inexpensive and fresh. But making pasta from scratch is time-consuming and difficult. The first product to try to break the compromise was dry pasta. Dry pasta costs more than homemade pasta and it is not as fresh, but it is much easier and faster to make.

The next run at the great pasta compromise was frozen pasta. Frozen pasta, which often comes in a microwavable container, is even quicker and easier to cook than dry pasta and requires little cleanup. But frozen pasta costs more than either homemade or dry pasta, and it is often less tasty.

In the mid-1980s, Contadina made its run at the great pasta compromise with the introduction of a fresh pasta product. Contadina's fresh pasta is twice the price of dry pasta and comes in a smaller package that doesn't serve as many people. It is five times more expensive per serving than dry pasta. Why, then, do people buy Contadina? Consumer research provides some interesting insights. Naturally, consumers like its freshness and its ease of cooking. More surprising is the fact that consumers are choosing Contadina over a meal at a restaurant. Before Contadina's fresh pasta became available, many people said they would never eat tortellini or ravioli at home, because preparing them from scratch was just too much trouble.

Breaking the great pasta compromise not only has made it easier to prepare good-tasting pasta at home, it also has upset the old trade-off between eating at home and going to a restaurant. In this context, Contadina makes a lot of sense. Consumers get the taste, variety, and freshness that can be found at restaurants, but in a product they can cook and eat at home for less money.

Often, when segment wide compromises imposed on consumers are broken, traditional trade-offs are

sidestepped and fundamental changes in the definition
of the business occur. This usually means a dramatic
shift in the set of relevant competitors. Because compromise breakers often find themselves competing against
companies that are higher cost and higher priced, they
are often able to grow rapidly and profitably by gaining
share from their new set of rivals. Contadina grew at
high double-digit rates to become a leader in fresh pas-
tas and sauces by the 1990s, with hundreds of millions of
dollars in sales.

A Breakthrough for Car Buyers

Breaking compromises between an entire industry and
its customers can release tremendous value. Circuit City,
best known in the United States as a big-box consumer-
electronics and appliance retailer, is a successful company, with sales growing at 26% per year and earnings at
30%. Its one major problem is that it is about to run out
of real estate. After opening stores in virtually all major
markets in the United States, Circuit City needs to go
somewhere else for fast-growth opportunities.

The retailer has found what it believes to be a
promising opportunity in an unlikely place—the used-
car business. In October 1993, Circuit City launched Car-
Max, a company whose strategy is to revolutionize the
way used cars are sold in the United States.

Selling used cars is a business with a stigma. In the
past, most people who bought used cars couldn't afford
new ones. The automakers, who naturally wanted to sell
new cars, reinforced the stigma. When Chrysler introduced its successful K-car in the early 1980s, Roger
Smith, then chairman of the board of General Motors

Corporation, was asked how GM would respond to the threat. Smith belittled the K-car by saying that "General Motors' answer to the Chrysler K-car is a two-year-old Oldsmobile."

This attitude toward used cars has not changed much. In the summer of 1995, a *Business Week* journalist grilled the program manager for the new Ford Taurus about the car's price. In frustration, the program manager responded that the 1996 Taurus was priced to sell 400,000 units a year. "If Joe Blow can't afford to buy a new car . . . let him buy a used car" (*Business Week*, July 24, 1995).

The used-car business may get no respect, but it should. Annual used-car sales in North America top $200 billion, making used cars the third-largest consumer category after food and clothing. In fact, there are more sales of used cars and light trucks than of new ones, and demand for used cars is growing faster. Moreover, the quality of used cars has risen with the rise in the quality of new cars.

Despite improvements in product quality, the business of selling used cars is virtually unchanged. A customer who opts for a used car faces many compromises. First, the buyer has to locate a car, usually by reviewing the classified advertisements in the local paper. Product variety is limited. In Toronto, for example, 20 to 30 used Tauruses are advertised for sale in the newspaper at any one time—from individuals, from dealers specializing in used cars, and from new-car dealers who also sell used cars. In the case of private sales, the buyer must call, make an appointment, and hope the seller will actually be there at the appointed time. The buyer must drive to see the car—which is unlikely to turn out to be the one the buyer wants or in good condition or priced reasonably or even still there: it could already have been sold.

When the buyer finds an attractive car, he or she can't expect to see any maintenance records. Some dealers certify their cars, but in Ontario, for example, certification means only that the glass is not cracked, that the lights and brakes work, that the exhaust does not leak, and that the tires have sufficient tread. In other words, certification guarantees only the bare necessities for roadworthiness.

Buyers of used cars, then, risk ending up owning a car with mechanical problems. Beyond this, they must endure a time-consuming and truly horrific buying process—more accurately, up to four processes: finding and buying the car, financing it, insuring it, and selling the old car. Buyers are at a disadvantage because knowledge about the product is asymmetrical: the seller knows more than the buyer.

Circuit City found a promising opportunity in an unlikely place: the used-car business.

Often the buyer is subjected to high-pressure sales tactics and forced to haggle over the price with salespeople whom he or she suspects are dishonest. And should problems arise, there is no clear recourse for the buyer.

The managers of Circuit City observed the size and growth of used-car sales and saw that many of the distinguishing capabilities of their own consumer-electronics business could break the compromises imposed on buyers of used cars.

Circuit City is known for its high variety of merchandise. CarMax takes the same approach. A typical large used-car dealer has only about 30 vehicles in stock. A large new-car dealer who sells used cars might have 130 vehicles. The first CarMax, in Richmond, Virginia, had 500 cars. The two stores that opened in Atlanta in August 1995 have 1,500 each.

CarMax further enhances customer choice by harnessing Circuit City's considerable systems capabilities. At CarMax, customers have access to computerized information through a kiosk that enables them to sort through the inventory of cars available not only at that site but at all the stores in the region. When CarMax advertises in any of the Richmond or Atlanta papers, it advertises inventory from both locations.

Unlike Circuit City, CarMax does not keep its inventory indoors. There is only one vehicle on display in the showroom, and it is fitted with arrows pointing to the 110 spots that have undergone performance and safety checks. The showroom's computerized kiosks provide information on the vehicles in stock, including their location on the lot. Should a customer be shopping with the family and want to see and drive a particular vehicle, CarMax provides a supervised day-care center for the children.

CarMax uses professional uniformed sales representatives, whose first job is to explain how to use the kiosk and then to help customers find the car they want. Car-Max prefers *not* to hire people with experience in selling new or used cars. Instead, it wants to hire presentable people whom it can train for two weeks (compare that with the minimal or nonexistent training that employees receive at new- and used-car dealers) and pay a set dollar amount per vehicle regardless of its selling price. This is an interesting departure from Circuit City's practice of paying a percentage-of-sales commission that encourages aggressive "selling up." CarMax did not want that pressure on its customers, so it designed an incentive system that eliminates the pressure on its sales representatives.

CarMax sets prices at below the average Blue Book value and offers no-haggle pricing and no-hassle guarantees. Every CarMax vehicle comes with the 110-point safety check and a 30-day warranty. For some cars, warranties of up to four years are available. In addition, CarMax customers have a five-day return guarantee: the car may be brought back with no questions asked as long as it has not been driven more than 250 miles.

Financing is available from NationsBank Corporation or from Circuit City's financing arm. Circuit City's financing tends to be for a longer term and usually requires lower deposits. Progressive Insurance will insure both the vehicle and the driver on the spot. People buying cars from CarMax can sell their old cars as well. The sale of the used car is a separate transaction from the purchase of a car. CarMax will buy any used car—although not at a price everyone will accept.

Driving Bottom-Line Growth at CarMax

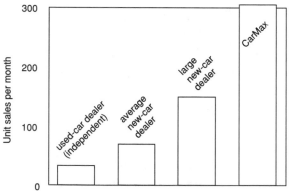

CarMax's innovative formula makes it possible to turn inventory much faster than is possible for traditional dealerships, thereby driving growth of the bottom line as well as growth of revenue.

The jury is still out on the success of CarMax. A host of imitators have emerged. Circuit City does not divulge the performance of its CarMax unit, but 4 stores were opened in 1995 and 90 more are planned by the year 2000. The race is on. Both used- and new-car dealers are likely to be bloodied. Historically, new-car dealers have sold about 80% of used cars that are less than four years old—CarMax's core offering. And those sales have accounted for anywhere from 35% to 65% of the dealers' profitability overall. (See the chart "Driving Bottom-Line Growth at CarMax.")

In addition, the sales of new cars are at risk. A popular saying in the automotive industry is that when you buy a new car and drive it off the lot, what you own is a very expensive used car. On average, the value of a new car plummets 28% in the first week after its sale. At CarMax, it is not uncommon to find current model-year vehicles with low mileage at substantially lower prices than those of new vehicles. In breaking so many of the compromises imposed on used-car buyers, CarMax may end the old trade-off between buying a used car and buying a new one.

CarMax is not the first to try to break the compromises imposed on used-car buyers. In northern New Jersey, there is a used-car dealership that has tackled the variety compromise by putting 600 cars on its lot and giving customers more choice. But this dealership has left everything else the same. Customers still have to haggle, obtain their financing and insurance from somewhere else, and dispose of their old car. Other dealers are touting no-haggle pricing. What sets CarMax apart is that it has put it all together: CarMax sells variety, it sells value, it sells convenience, it promises that you can be in and out in 90 minutes with a car, and it delivers a comfortable experience. Many of the car dealers near

CarMax locations are matching CarMax on price, and they think, mistakenly, that the job is done. It's not. People want a different buying experience and they're getting it from CarMax.

Finding Opportunities in Any Business

Growth strategies built around the idea of breaking compromises are neither new nor limited to a few particular industries. But to visualize such a strategy requires a company's managers to clear their heads of the conventional thinking that pervades their industry. The Charles Schwab Corporation has grown steadily over two decades by breaking one industry compromise after another.

Schwab began as a discount stockbrokerage in 1975, when U.S. equity markets were deregulated and price competition on stock-trading commissions was introduced. Discount brokers ended a major compromise for individual investors, who had hitherto been forced to put up with high prices if they wanted to buy and sell securities.

Schwab, however, saw that the discount brokerage segment was itself imposing new compromises. Customers who opted for a low price worried about service reliability. Schwab tackled the problem head-on, first by investing heavily in computer technology that allowed almost immediate confirmation of orders over the telephone. At the time, even Merrill Lynch & Company could not do that. Schwab also invested in the firm's brand name and in retail offices, both of which instilled confidence in consumers. In the process, the firm broke the compromise between price and reliable service and grew dramatically through the early 1980s.

Schwab saw that other compromises remained to be broken. In exchange for low prices, customers had been compromised on convenience, flexibility, and ease of transferring funds. In the early 1980s, Schwab pioneered 24-hour-a-day, seven-day-a-week service. It introduced the Schwab One cash-management account with Visa card and checking privileges, copying a Merrill Lynch product but eliminating the need to deal with a full-commission broker. Schwab also pioneered automated phone trading and eventually electronic trading directly from the customer's personal computer.

Over time, Schwab's management realized that the company was no longer a simple discount broker but in fact a broad, value-priced provider of cash, stocks, bonds, and mutual funds. The compromises Schwab had broken had generated a 20% to 25% per year growth rate and made Schwab the largest non-full-commission broker in the United States. But Schwab was ready to break yet another compromise to fuel its next stage of growth.

Until 1992, most consumers wanting to buy mutual funds had been forced to choose among different fund companies, each of which serviced its own accounts. Because diversification and high performance were not easily accomplished within a single family of funds, many consumers placed money with a number of different fund-management companies. Most investors were frustrated by the complexity of dealing with different statements, different rules, and different sales representatives.

In 1992, Schwab changed the scenario by introducing OneSource, a single point of purchase for more than 350 no-load mutual funds in 50 different fund families. One-Source gives customers a single account with one monthly statement that tracks the performance of all their funds. There are no transaction fees on OneSource accounts, so customers can shift their money among different fund families without any charge. Schwab can do this because it is paid directly by the funds as their sales representative and subaccount processor.

OneSource has grown to include 500 mutual funds, driving Schwab's mutual-fund assets from $6 billion in 1991 to more than $60 billion in 1996 and making it the third-largest mutual-fund distributor in the United States. No longer forced to compromise on assortment, price, and convenience, consumers have been flocking to OneSource to manage their investments.

Schwab's experience illustrates that relentless breaking of compromises can be a source for continuing growth. In fact, there are at least seven ways in which companies can find and exploit compromise-breaking opportunities in any industry.

Shop the way the customer shops. At Schwab, the most important source of ongoing insight is employees who use the company's products and services just as Schwab's customers do. For example, the belief that customers would value the convenience of 24-hour-a-day, seven-day-a-week systems was heavily supported by Schwab's own employees, who wanted that kind of flexibility in managing their own investments. Unfortunately, in many industries, executives never know how customers shop. In the auto industry, executives of the Big Three do not buy cars. Their secretaries do it for them, over the telephone. The cars are delivered to the executives clean, full of gas, and ready to go. For most Big Three executives, buying a car the way ordinary customers do would be an out-of-body experience.

Pay careful attention to how the customer really uses the product or service. In all industries, people exhibit *compensatory behaviors.* They devise their own ways of using the product or service to compensate for the fact that if they did only what the company intended them to do, they wouldn't really get what they wanted. In every product category, consumers can undertake dozens of compensatory behaviors, and each of those can have significant compromise-breaking potential.

In the brokerage business, it was common knowledge that customers often called back a second or even a third time to confirm that their trade had gone through at the price they had requested. Schwab paid careful attention to customers' actual behavior and realized that the ability to provide immediate confirmation at the time an order was taken would eliminate those second and third calls—saving customers a lot of trouble and giving Schwab a significant advantage over other brokers.

Explore customers' latent dissatisfactions. Most companies ask their customers to describe their dissatisfactions with existing products and services. Such surveys usually lead to helpful improvements, but truly significant breakthroughs are generally the result of tapping into much deeper dissatisfactions. Those can be called *latent dissatisfactions* because consumers are unable to articulate their unhappiness with the product or service category. Chrysler's development of the minivan, for example, tapped into latent dissatisfaction with both station

Chrysler's development of the minivan tapped into latent dissatisfaction with both station wagons and full-size vans.

wagons and full-size vans. Station wagons couldn't carry enough and were hard to load and unload. Full-size vans were more useful, but they were not fun to drive. Minivans broke the compromise by "cubing out" the box design of the station wagon. Ford Motor Company and GM had both researched customers' feelings about station wagons and had found that they could meet obvious needs with features such as two-way doors, electric rear windows, and third seats. But they did not explore the "white space" between station wagons (based on car platforms) and vans (based on truck platforms). The minivan—a van based on a car platform—was hidden in this white space defined by customers' latent dissatisfactions.

Look for uncommon denominators. Over time, companies tend to drift toward providing products or services that, on average, meet the needs of large numbers of customers. But compromises often lurk in this common-denominator approach. Schwab, for example, has now separated the service channel for the high-volume equity trader from that for the ordinary investor, whose needs are simpler. Each receives different services and pays different fees.

Some companies are reluctant to abandon the approach of averaging costs across all customers, because they believe abandoning it will reduce the profitability of their high-volume accounts. But recent history suggests that if managers don't separate out what should be discrete businesses, a new or existing rival will do it for them. Recognition of that fact begets a relentless search for new compromises to break.

Pay careful attention to anomalies. Anomalies often are a rich source for compromise breaking. The one regional sales office that significantly outperforms all others and for which there is no obvious explanation; the factory that appears to have a scale disadvantage but still has a lower production cost; the supplier who has lower cost and higher quality despite having an older product design: those anomalies are all worth exploring as potential compromise-breaking opportunities.

In Schwab's case, the idea of creating local offices grew out of an anomaly. Charles Schwab's uncle was looking for a business to run and Schwab decided to open an office in Sacramento, California, to give his uncle something to do. At the time, offices were seen as unnecessary and costly overhead for discount brokerage firms.

Subsequently, Schwab noticed that Sacramento was significantly outperforming other cities that had no offices. There was no obvious explanation. By exploring this anomaly carefully, Schwab discovered that retail sales offices had a number of important advantages even for a firm that typically dealt with customers by telephone. Local offices provided a rich source of customer leads through walk-in traffic and reassured those new customers who had concerns about trusting a broker they had heard of only from television. The offices provided a sense of solidity and a place customers could go to transact business. Schwab discovered that even in a high-tech age, customers like knowing that there is an office down the street or at least across town. Fully probing this anomaly led Schwab to build a large retail network.

Look for diseconomies in the industry's value chain. Today, in industry after industry, companies are innovating the management of their value chain in ways that are more rewarding for consumers. When the Schwab firm entered the mutual fund business, its first thought was to create its own family of funds. Careful analysis of the industry value chain, however, revealed a bigger opportunity. Only a handful of the largest companies had sufficient economies of scale to distribute their funds cost-effectively—and those companies lost the ability to talk directly to their individual customers. Schwab's solution was to become an intermediary between its own customer base and a large number of subscale mutual-fund companies. Through OneSource, the firm served the needs of the fund companies and at the same time interposed itself between the funds and the customer. Schwab's ownership of the direct customer relationship can now provide a platform for growth in other financial services, such as insurance.

Look for analogous solutions to the industry's compromises. Some of the best compromise-breaking ideas are probably already out there—in someone else's industry. Circuit City's CarMax borrows many practices from other retail sectors. For example, its idea of offering extended warranties on used cars is borrowed from appliance and consumer-electronics retailing. To keep inventory moving and selection fresh, CarMax has copied a practice used commonly in soft-goods retailing—automatically discounting inventory as it ages. CarMax's practice of offering flat sales commissions and its low-pressure selling tactics can be observed in a number of sectors. Best Buy Company, one of Circuit City's competitors in electronics retailing, uses that approach to create the kind of low-key, self-serve environment CarMax was looking for.

An Organizing Principle for Growth

Many companies today are searching for growth. But how and where should they look? Managers will often turn first to line extensions, geographic expansion, or acquisitions. In the right circumstances, each of those makes sense. But we believe that innovations that break fundamental compromises in a business are far more powerful.

Breaking compromises can, in fact, provide an organizing principle for the pursuit of growth. The CEO of a large financial-services company asked his initially skeptical management team to specify and value all the compromises imposed on its customers. The exercise was eye opening.

To get its employees to focus their energies on compromise breaking, a company should start by asking them to immerse themselves in the customer's experience. It is critical to develop a strong, almost visceral feel for the compromises consumers experience. Whirlpool Corporation, the $8 billion appliance maker, identified a specific individual who personified the compromises all its customers bore.

Whirlpool's market research showed consumers to be generally satisfied with the home appliances they owned. But digging deeper, Whirlpool discovered a reservoir of latent dissatisfaction with all the activities for which the appliances were used—doing laundry, preparing food, cleaning up after meals. Although consumers didn't expect a lot more of their washing machines, ranges, and dishwashers, they were nevertheless very dissatisfied with household chores.

Those latent dissatisfactions became the basis for Whirlpool's brand strategy. In 1992, after decades of competing mostly on cost with companies such as General Electric, Whirlpool wanted to build a new and more profitable strategy around a more sharply differentiated brand. Management knew it needed to articulate the strategy and mobilize all employees behind a vision. Someone at Whirlpool saw an interview on a national television-news program with an overworked woman named Gail and taped it, recognizing Gail as the embodiment of Whirlpool's target customer. Gail was a 40-year-old woman taking care of several children at home while holding down a full-time job. Gail did all the cooking, the laundry, and the housework. Her husband's role was apparently restricted to playing sports with the children and helping them with their homework. The image was consistent with Whirlpool's research, which showed that women in the United States who work as many hours as their husbands in jobs outside the home continue to do most of the household chores as well. Gail personified the pressed-for-time working woman.

At the end of the video clip, the interviewer turns to her and says, "You're taking care of everyone in this family. Who takes care of you?" Before she can reply, her husband answers for her, "I take care of Gail." Gail shoots him a look that could kill.

The video, which became a rallying point for Whirlpool's new strategy, challenged all employees to think about how Whirlpool could be the company that takes care of Gail. Why, for example, was it taking Gail so long to clean up after meals? The traditional stove top was obviously designed by someone who was spared the daily responsibility of keeping it clean. The top of Whirlpool's CleanTop stove is completely flat, eliminating all the grease traps of the old design. Dishwashers used to be deafening, but now Gail can work on her kitchen computer while Whirlpool's Quiet Partner dishwasher is running.

More compromises wait to be broken. Why is doing the laundry such a chore? Gail's washing machine takes less time than her dryer to complete its cycle. Gail compensates by starting with lighter, faster-drying loads first. But eventually the process bogs down, and Gail is wasting time and energy running to the basement because no one makes a synchronized washer and dryer.

Breaking compromises can be a powerful organizing principle to enlist an entire organization in thinking about growth. The lesson from all the high-growth compromise breakers we've observed is this: The opportunity to identify and exploit compromises for faster growth and improved profitability is there for the taking. But managers must go to customers and look for themselves. This isn't a job that can be delegated to the market research department. Managers must ask themselves why customers behave the way they do. An auto dealer told us how proud he was of his expansive, well-lit lot with no fences. "My customers like to come after hours to look at cars and trucks," he proclaimed. He apparently never asked himself why they would do such a strange thing. And it never occurred to him that they might be looking at cars after hours precisely because they didn't want to have to deal with *him*.

To find the kinds of growth opportunities companies like CarMax, Schwab, and Contadina are pursuing, managers have to get inside the customer's skin and ask, What compromises am I putting up with? What's wrong with this picture? Where's the minivan in this company?

Originally published in September–October 1996
Reprint 96507

What comparisons do customers make in Terced?

> forced to buy software & maintenance & service
> forced to work w/ their IT departments
> customers carry the risk of their implementation
> compiles carry the the functionality risk of their products
> software cannot be re-sold; it is a non-transferable asset
> compiles what are the trade-offs for Terced SaaS?

      > cost   > availability   > risk / predictability
      > expertise   > speed of use   > hidden costs

> we compete against IT vs. customers
> why does the sales process take so long?

Value Innovation

The Strategic Logic of High Growth

W. CHAN KIM AND RENÉE MAUBORGNE

Executive Summary

WHY ARE SOME COMPANIES able to sustain high growth in revenues and profits—and others are not? To answer that question, the authors, both of INSEAD, spent five years studying more than 30 companies around the world. They found that the difference between the high-growth companies and their less successful competitors was in each group's assumptions about strategy. Managers of the less successful companies followed conventional strategic logic. Managers of the high-growth companies followed what the authors call the *logic of value innovation*.

Conventional strategic logic and value innovation differ along the basic dimensions of strategy. Many companies take their industry's conditions as given; value innovators don't. Many companies let competitors set the parameters of their strategic thinking; value

25

innovators do not use rivals as benchmarks. Rather than focus on the differences among customers, value innovators look for what customers value in common. Rather than view opportunities through the lens of existing assets and capabilities, value innovators ask, What if we start anew?

The authors tell the story of the French hotelier Accor, which discarded the notion of what a hotel is supposed to look like in order to offer what most customers want: a good night's sleep at a low price. And Virgin Atlantic challenged industry conventions by eliminating first-class service and channeling savings into innovations for business-class passengers. Those companies didn't set out to build advantages over the competition, but they ended up achieving the greatest competitive advantages.

AFTER A DECADE OF DOWNSIZING AND INCREAS-INGLY INTENSE COMPETITION, profitable growth is a tremendous challenge many companies face. Why do some companies achieve sustained high growth in both revenues and profits? In a five-year study of high-growth companies and their less successful competitors, we found that the answer lies in the way each group approached strategy. The difference in approach was not a matter of managers choosing one analytical tool or planning model over another. The difference was in the companies' fundamental, implicit assumptions about strategy. The less successful companies took a conventional approach: their strategic thinking was dominated by the idea of staying ahead of the competition. In stark contrast, the high-growth companies paid little attention to matching or beating

their rivals. Instead, they sought to make their competitors irrelevant through a strategic logic we call
value innovation. (See "Researching the Roots of High
Growth," on page 50.)

Consider Bert Claeys, a Belgian company that oper-
ates movie theaters. From the 1960s to the 1980s, the
movie theater industry in Belgium was declining
steadily. With the spread of videocassette recorders and
satellite and cable television, the average Belgian's
moviegoing dropped from eight to two times per year.
By the 1980s, many cinema operators (COs) were forced
to shut down.

The COs that remained found themselves competing
head-to-head for a shrinking market. All took similar
actions. They turned cinemas into multiplexes with as
many as ten screens, broadened their film offerings to
attract all customer segments, expanded their food and
drink services, and increased showing times.

Those attempts to leverage existing assets became
irrelevant in 1988, when Bert Claeys created Kinepolis.
Neither an ordinary cinema nor a multiplex, Kinepolis is
the world's first megaplex, with 25 screens and 7,600
seats. By offering moviegoers a radically superior experience, Kinepolis won 50% of the market in Brussels in its
first year and expanded the market by about 40%. Today
many Belgians refer not to a night at the movies but to
an evening at Kinepolis.

Consider the differences between Kinepolis and other
Belgian movie theaters. The typical Belgian multiplex
has small viewing rooms that often have no more than
100 seats, screens that measure 7 meters by 5 meters,
and 35-millimeter projection equipment. Viewing rooms
at Kinepolis have up to 700 seats, and there is so much
legroom that viewers do not have to move when some-

one passes by. Bert Claeys installed oversized seats with individual armrests and designed a steep slope in the floor to ensure everyone an unobstructed view. At Kinepolis, screens measure up to 29 meters by 10 meters and rest on their own foundations so that sound vibrations are not transmitted from one screen to another. Many viewing rooms have 70-millimeter projection equipment and state-of-the-art sound equipment. And Bert Claeys challenged the industry's conventional wisdom about the importance of prime, city-center real estate by locating Kinepolis off the ring road circling Brussels, 15 minutes from downtown. Patrons park for free in large, well-lit lots. The company was prepared to lose out on foot traffic in order to solve a major problem for the majority of moviegoers in Brussels: the scarcity and high cost of parking.

Bert Claeys can offer this radically superior cinema experience without increasing the price of tickets because the concept of the megaplex results in one of the lowest cost structures in the industry. The average cost to build a seat at Kinepolis is about 70,000 Belgian francs, less than half the industry's average in Brussels. Why? The megaplex's location outside the city is cheaper; its size gives it economies in purchasing, more leverage with film distributors, and better overall margins; and with 25 screens served by a central ticketing and lobby area, Kinepolis achieves economies in personnel and overhead. Furthermore, the company spends very little on advertising because its value innovation generates a lot of word-of-mouth praise.

Within its supposedly unattractive industry, Kinepolis has achieved spectacular growth and profits. Belgian moviegoers now go to the cinema more frequently because of Kinepolis, and people who never went to the

How Kinepolis Achieves Profitable Growth

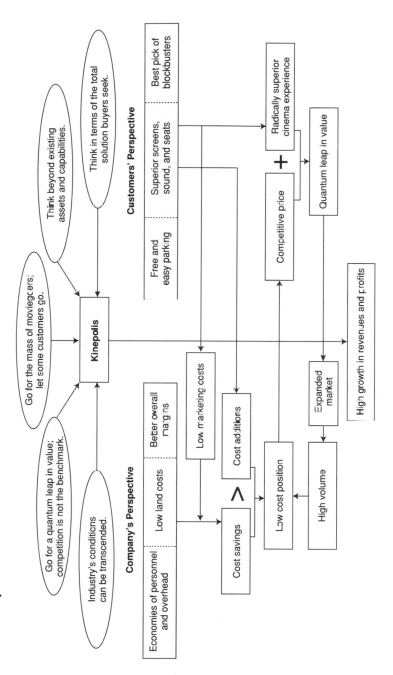

movies have been drawn into the market. Instead of battling competitors over targeted segments of the market, Bert Claeys made the competition irrelevant. (See the chart "How Kinepolis Achieves Profitable Growth.")

Why did other Belgian COs fail to seize that opportunity? Like the others, Bert Claeys was an incumbent with sunk investments: a network of cinemas across Belgium. In fact, Kinepolis would have represented a smaller investment for some COs than it did for Bert Claeys. Most COs were thinking—implicitly or explicitly—along these lines: The industry is shrinking, so we should not make major investments—especially in fixed assets. But we can improve our performance by outdoing our competitors on each of the key dimensions of competition. We must have better films, better services, and better marketing.

Bert Claeys followed a different strategic logic. The company set out to make its cinema experience not better than that at competitors' theaters but completely different—and irresistible. The company thought as if it were a new entrant to the market. It sought to reach the mass of moviegoers by focusing on widely shared needs. In order to give most moviegoers a package they would value highly, the company put aside conventional thinking about what a theater is supposed to look like. And the company did all that while reducing its costs. That's the logic behind value innovation.

Conventional Logic Versus Value Innovation

Conventional strategic logic and the logic of value innovation differ along the five basic dimensions of strategy. Those differences determine which questions managers ask, what opportunities they see and pursue, and how they understand risk. (See the table "Two Strategic Logics.")

INDUSTRY ASSUMPTIONS

Many companies take their industry's conditions as given and set strategy accordingly. Value innovators don't. No matter how the rest of the industry is faring, value innovators look for blockbuster ideas and quantum leaps in value. Had Bert Claeys, for example, taken its industry's conditions as given, it would never have created a megaplex. The company would have followed the endgame strategy of milking its business or the zero-sum strategy of competing for share in a shrinking market. Instead, through Kinepolis, the company transcended the industry's conditions.

STRATEGIC FOCUS

Many companies let competitors set the parameters of their strategic thinking. They compare their strengths and weaknesses with those of their competitors and focus on building advantages. Consider this example. For years, the major U.S. television networks used the same format for news programming. All aired shows in the same time slot and competed on their analysis of events, the professionalism with which they delivered the news, and the popularity of their anchors. In 1980, CNN came on the scene with a focus on creating a quantum leap in value, not on competing with the networks. CNN replaced the networks' format with real-time news from around the world 24 hours a day. CNN not only emerged as the leader in global news broadcasting—and

Two Strategic Logics

The Five Dimensions of Strategy	Conventional Logic	Value Innovation Logic
Industry Assumptions	Industry's conditions are given.	Industry's conditions can be shaped.
Strategic Focus	A company should build competitive advantages. The aim is to beat the competition.	Competition is not the benchmark. A company should pursue a quantum leap in value to dominate the market.
Customers	A company should retain and expand its customer base through further segmentation and customization. It should focus on the differences in what customers value.	A value innovator targets the mass of buyers and willingly lets some existing customers go. It focuses on the key commonalities in what customers value.
Assets and Capabilities	A company should leverage its existing assets and capabilities.	A company must not be constrained by what it already has. It must ask, What would we do if we were starting anew?
Product and Service Offerings	An industry's traditional boundaries determine the products and services a company offers. The goal is to maximize the value of those offerings.	A value innovator thinks in terms of the total solution customers seek, even if that takes the company beyond its industry's traditional offerings.

created new demand around the world—but also was able to produce 24 hours of real-time news for one-fifth the cost of 1 hour of network news.

Conventional logic leads companies to compete at the margin for incremental share. The logic of value innovation starts with an ambition to dominate the market by offering a tremendous leap in value. Value innovators never say, Here's what competitors are doing; let's do this in response. They monitor competitors but do not use them as benchmarks. Hasso Plattner, vice chairman of SAP, the global leader in business-application software, puts it this way: "I'm not interested in whether we are better than the competition. The real test is, will most buyers still seek out our products even if we don't market them?"

Because value innovators do not focus on competing, they can distinguish the factors that deliver superior value from all the factors the industry competes on. They do not expend their resources to offer certain product and service features just because that is what their rivals are doing. CNN, for example, decided not to compete with the networks in the race to get big name anchors. Companies that follow the logic of value innovation free up their resources to identify and deliver completely new sources of value. Ironically, value innovators do not set out to build advantages over the competition, but they end up achieving the greatest competitive advantages.

CUSTOMERS

Many companies seek growth through retaining and expanding their customer bases. This often leads to finer segmentation and greater customization of offerings to meet specialized needs. Value innovation follows a different logic. Instead of focusing on the differences among customers, value innovators build on the powerful commonalities in the features that customers value. In the words of a senior executive at the French hotelier Accor, "We focus on what unites customers. Customers' differences often prevent you from seeing what's most important." Value innovators believe that most people will put their differences aside if they are offered a considerable increase in value. Those companies shoot for the core of the market, even if it means that they lose some of their customers.

ASSETS AND CAPABILITIES

Many companies view business opportunities through the lens of their existing assets and capabilities. They ask, Given what we have, what is the best we can do? In contrast, value innovators ask, What if we start anew? That is the question the British company Virgin Group put to itself in the late 1980s. The company had a sizable chain of small music stores across the United Kingdom when it came up with the idea of megastores for music and entertainment, which would offer customers a tremendous leap in value. Seeing that its small stores could not be leveraged to seize that opportunity, the company decided to sell off the entire chain. As one of Virgin's executives puts it, "We don't let what we can do today condition our view of what it takes to win tomorrow. We take a clean-slate approach."

This is not to say that value innovators never leverage their existing assets and capabilities. They often do. But, more important, they assess business opportunities without being biased or constrained by where they are at a given moment. For that reason, value innovators not only have more insight into where value for buyers resides—and how it is changing—but also are much more likely to act on that insight.

PRODUCT AND SERVICE OFFERINGS

Conventional competition takes place within clearly established boundaries defined by the products and services the industry traditionally offers. Value innovators often cross those boundaries. They think in terms of the total solution buyers seek, and they try to overcome the chief compromises their industry forces customers to make—as Bert Claeys did by providing free parking. A senior executive at Compaq Computer describes the approach: "We continually ask where our products and services fit in the total chain of buyers' solutions. We seek to solve buyers' major problems across the entire chain, even if that takes us into a new business. We are not limited by the industry's definition of what we should and should not do."

Creating a New Value Curve

How does the logic of value innovation translate into a company's offerings in the marketplace? Consider the case of Accor. In the mid-1980s, the budget hotel industry in France was suffering from stagnation and overcapacity. Accor's cochairmen, Paul Dubrule and Gérard Pélisson, challenged the company's managers to create a quantum leap in value for customers. The managers were urged to forget everything they knew about the existing rules, practices, and traditions of the industry. They were asked what they would do if Accor were starting fresh.

In 1985, when Accor launched Formule 1, a line of budget hotels, there were two distinct market segments in the budget hotel industry. One segment consisted of no-star and one-star hotels, whose average price per room was between 60 and 90 French francs. Customers came to those hotels just for the low price. The other segment was two-star hotels, with an average price of 200 francs per room. Those more expensive hotels attracted customers by offering a better sleeping environment than the no-star and one-star hotels. People had come to expect that they would get what they paid for: either they would pay more and get a decent night's sleep or they would pay less and put up with poor beds and noise.

Accor's managers began by identifying what customers of all budget hotels—no-star, one-star, and two-star—wanted: a good night's sleep for a low price. Focusing on those widely shared needs, Accor's managers saw the opportunity to overcome the chief compromise that the industry forced customers to make. They asked themselves the following four questions:

- Which of the factors that our industry takes for granted should be eliminated?

- Which factors should be reduced well below the industry's standard?

- Which factors should be raised well above the industry's standard?

- Which factors should be created that the industry has never offered?

The first question forces managers to consider whether the factors that companies compete on actually deliver value to consumers. Often those factors are taken for granted, even though they have no value or even detract from value. Sometimes what buyers value changes fundamentally, but companies that are focused on benchmarking one another do not act on—or even perceive—the change. The second question forces managers to determine whether products and services have been overdesigned in the race to match and beat the competition. The third question pushes managers to uncover and eliminate the compromises their industry forces customers to make. The fourth question helps managers break out of the industry's established boundaries to discover entirely new sources of value for consumers.

In answering the questions, Accor came up with a new concept for a hotel, which led to the launch of Formule 1. First, the company eliminated such standard hotel features as costly restaurants and appealing lounges. Accor reckoned that even though it might lose some customers, most people would do without those features.

Accor's managers believed that budget hotels were overserving customers along other dimensions as well. On those, Formule 1 offers less than many no-star hotels do. For example, receptionists are on hand only during peak check-in and check-out hours. At all other times, customers use an automated teller. Rooms at a Formule 1 hotel are small and equipped only with a bed and bare necessities—no stationery, desks, or decorations. Instead of closets and dressers, there are a few shelves and a pole for clothing in one corner of the room. The rooms themselves are modular blocks manufactured in a factory—a method that results in economies of scale in production, high quality control, and good sound insulation.

Formule 1 gives Accor considerable cost advantages. The company cut in half the average cost of building a room, and its staff costs dropped from between 25% and 35% of sales—the industry's average—to between 20% and 23%. Those cost savings have allowed Accor to improve the features customers value most to levels beyond those of the average French two-star hotel, but the price is only marginally above that of one-star hotels.

Customers have rewarded Accor for its value innovation. The company has not only captured the mass of French budget-hotel customers but also expanded the market. From truck drivers who previously slept in their vehicles to businesspeople needing a few hours of rest, new customers have been drawn to the budget category. Formule 1 made the competition irrelevant. At last count, Formule 1's market share in France was greater than the sum of the five next-largest players.

The extent of Accor's departure from the conventional logic of its industry can be seen in what we call a *value curve*—a graphic depiction of a company's relative performance across its industry's key success factors. (See the graph "Formule 1's Value Curve.") According to the conventional logic of competition, an industry's value curve follows one basic shape. Rivals try to improve value by offering a little more for a little less, but most don't challenge the shape of the curve.

Like Accor, all the high-performing companies we studied created fundamentally new and superior value curves. They achieved that by a combination of eliminating features, creating features, and reducing and raising others to levels unprecedented in their industries. Take, for example, SAP, a business-application-software company that was started in the early 1970s by five former IBM employees in Walldorf, Germany, and became the worldwide industry leader. Until the 1980s, business-application-software makers focused on subsegmenting the market and customizing their offerings to meet buyers' functional needs, such as production management, logistics, human resources, and payroll.

While most software companies were focusing on improving the performance of particular application products, SAP took aim at the mass of buyers. Instead of competing on customers' differences, SAP sought out important commonalities in what customers value. The

Formule 1's Value Curve

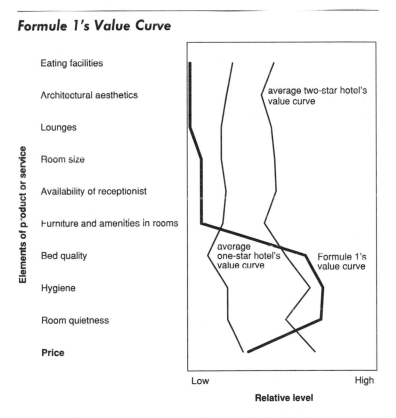

Formule 1 offers unprecedented value to the mass of budget hotel customers in France by giving them much more of what they need most and much less of what they are willing to do without.

company correctly hypothesized that for most customers, the performance advantages of highly customized, individual software modules had been overestimated. Such modules forfeited the efficiency and information advantages of an integrated system, which allows real-time data exchange across a company.

In 1979, SAP launched R/2, a line of real-time, integrated business-application software for mainframe computers. R/2 has no restriction on the platform of the host hardware; buyers can capitalize on the best hardware available and reduce their maintenance costs dramatically. Most important, R/2 leads to huge gains in accuracy and efficiency because a company needs to enter its data only once. And R/2 improves the flow of information. A sales manager, for example, can find out when a product will be delivered and why it is late by cross-referencing the production database. SAP's growth and profits have exceeded its industry's. In 1992, SAP achieved a new value innovation with R/3, a line of software for the client-server market.

The Trap of Competing, the Necessity of Repeating

What happens once a company has created a new value curve? Sooner or later, the competition tries to imitate it. In many industries, value innovators do not face a credible challenge for many years, but in others, rivals appear more quickly. Eventually, however, a value innovator will find its growth and profits under attack. Too often, in an attempt to defend its hard-earned customer base, the company launches offenses. But the imitators often persist, and the value innovator—despite its best intentions—may end up in a race to beat the competition. Obsessed with hanging on to market share, the company may fall into the trap of conventional strategic logic. If the company doesn't find its way out of the trap, the basic shape of its value curve will begin to look just like those of its rivals.

Consider the following example. When Compaq Computer launched its first personal computer in 1983, most PC buyers were sophisticated corporate users and technology enthusiasts. IBM had defined the industry's value curve. Compaq's first offering—the first IBM-compatible PC—represented a completely new value curve. Compaq's product not only was technologically superb but also was priced roughly 15% below IBM's. Within three years of its start-up, Compaq joined the *Fortune* 500. No other company had ever achieved that status as quickly.

How did IBM respond? It tried to match and beat Compaq's value curve. And Compaq, determined to defend itself, became focused on beating IBM. But while IBM and Compaq were battling over feature enhancements, most buyers were becoming more sensitive to price. User-friendliness was becoming more important to customers than the latest technology. Compaq's focus on competing with IBM led the company to produce a line of PCs that were overengineered and overpriced for most buyers. When IBM walked off the cliff in the late 1980s, Compaq was following close behind.

Could Compaq have foreseen the need to create another value innovation rather than go head-to-head against IBM? If Compaq had monitored the industry's value curves, it would have realized that by the mid to late 1980s, IBM's and other PC makers' value curves were converging with its own. And by the late 1980s, the curves were nearly identical. That should have been the signal to Compaq that it was time for another quantum leap.

Monitoring value curves may also keep a company from pursuing innovation when there is still a huge profit stream to be collected from its current offering. In some rapidly emerging industries, companies must innovate frequently. In many other industries, companies can harvest their successes for a long time: a radically different value curve is difficult for incumbents to imitate, and the volume advantages that come with value innovation make imitation costly. Kinepolis, Formule 1, and CNN, for example, have enjoyed uncontested dominance for a long time. CNN's value innovation was not challenged for almost ten years. Yet we have seen companies pursue novelty for novelty's sake, driven by internal pressures to leverage unique competencies or to apply the latest technology. Value innovation is about offering unprecedented value, not technology or competencies. It is not the same as being first to market.

When a company's value curve is fundamentally different from that of the rest of the industry—and the difference is valued by most customers—managers should resist innovation. Instead, companies should embark on geographic expansion and operational improvements to achieve maximum economies of scale and market coverage. That approach discourages imitation and allows companies to tap the potential of their current value innovation. Bert Claeys, for example, has been rapidly rolling out and improving its Kinepolis concept with Metropolis, a megaplex in Antwerp, and with megaplexes in many countries in Europe and Asia. And Accor has already built more than 300 Formule 1 hotels across Europe, Africa, and Australia. The company is now targeting Asia.

The Three Platforms

The companies we studied that were most successful at repeating value innovation were those that took advantage of all three platforms on which value innovation can take place: product, service, and delivery. The precise meaning of the three platforms varies across industries and companies, but, in general, the product platform is the physical product; the service platform is support such as maintenance, customer service, warranties, and training for distributors and retailers; and the delivery platform includes logistics and the channel used to deliver the product to customers.

Too often, managers trying to create a value innovation focus on the product platform and ignore the other two. Over time, that approach is not likely to yield many opportunities for repeated value innovation. As customers and technologies change, each platform presents new possibilities. Just as good farmers rotate their crops, good value innovators rotate their value platforms. (See "Virgin Atlantic: Flying in the Face of Conventional Logic," on page 51.)

The story of Compaq's server business, which was part of the company's successful comeback, illustrates how the three platforms can be used alternately over time to create new value curves. (See the graph "How Has Compaq Stayed on Top of the Server Industry?") In late 1989, Compaq introduced its first server, the SystemPro, which was designed to run five network operating systems—SCO UNIX, OS/2, Vines, NetWare, and DOS—and many application programs. Like the SystemPro, most servers could handle many operating systems and application programs. Compaq observed, however,

How Has Compaq Stayed on Top of the Server Industry?

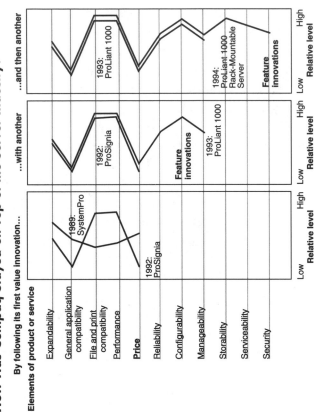

By following its first value innovation... ...with another ...and then another

Elements of product or service

Expandability
General application compatibility
File and print compatibility
Performance
Price
Reliability
Configurability
Manageability
Storability
Serviceability
Security

1989: SystemPro
1992: ProSignia

1992: ProSignia
Feature innovations
1993: ProLiant 1000

1993: ProLiant 1000
1994: ProLiant 1000 Rack-Mountable Server
Feature innovations

Low   Relative level   High
Low   Relative level   High
Low   Relative level   High

that the majority of customers used only a small fraction of a server's capacity. After identifying the needs that cut across the mass of users, Compaq decided to build a radically simplified server that would be optimized to run NetWare and file and print only. Launched in 1992, the ProSignia was a value innovation on the product platform. The new server gave buyers twice the System-Pro's file-and-print performance at one-third the price. Compaq achieved that value innovation mainly by reducing general application compatibility—a reduction that translated into much lower manufacturing costs.

As competitors tried to imitate the ProSignia and value curves in the industry began to converge, Compaq took another leap, this time from the service platform. Viewing its servers not as stand-alone products but as elements of its customers' total computing needs, Compaq saw that 90% of customers' costs were in servicing networks and only 10% were in the server hardware itself. Yet Compaq, like other companies in the industry, had been focusing on maximizing the price-performance ratio of the server hardware, the least costly element for buyers.

Compaq redeployed its resources to bring out the ProLiant 1000, a server that incorporates two innovative pieces of software. The first, SmartStart, configures server hardware and network information to suit a company's operating system and application programs. It slashes the time it takes a customer to configure a server network and makes installation virtually error-free so that servers perform reliably from day one. The second piece of software, Insight Manager, helps customers manage their server networks by, for example, spotting overheating boards or troubled disk drives before they break down.

By innovating on the service platform, Compaq created a superior value curve and expanded its market. Companies lacking expertise in information technology had been skeptical of their ability to configure and manage a network server. SmartStart and Insight Manager helped put those companies at ease. The ProLiant 1000 came out a winner.

As more and more companies acquired servers, Compaq observed that its customers often lacked the space to store the equipment properly. Stuffed into closets or left on the floor with tangled wires, expensive servers were often damaged, were certainly not secure, and were difficult to service.

By focusing on customer value—not on competitors—Compaq saw that it was time for another value innovation on the product platform. The company introduced the ProLiant 1000 Rack-Mountable Server, which allows companies to store servers in a tall, lean cabinet in a central location. The product makes efficient use of space and ensures that machines are protected and are easy to monitor, repair, and enhance. Compaq designed the rack mount to fit both its products and those of other manufacturers, thus attracting even more buyers and discouraging imitation. The company's sales and profits rose again as its new value curve diverged from the industry's.

Compaq is now looking to the delivery platform for a value innovation that will dramatically reduce the lead time between a customer's order and the arrival of the equipment. Lead times have forced customers to forecast their needs—a difficult task—and have often required them to patch together costly solutions while waiting for their orders to be filled. Now that servers are widely used and the demands placed on them are multiplying rapidly, Compaq believes that shorter lead times will provide a quantum leap in value for customers. The company is currently working on a delivery option that will permit its products to be built to customers' specifications and shipped within 48 hours of the order. That value innovation will allow Compaq to reduce its inventory costs and minimize the accumulation of outdated stock.

By achieving value innovations on all three platforms, Compaq has been able to maintain a gap between its value curve and those of other players. Despite the pace of competition in its industry, Compaq's repeated value innovations are allowing the company to remain the number one maker of servers worldwide. Since the company's turnaround, overall sales and profits have almost quadrupled.

Driving a Company for High Growth

One of the most striking findings of our research is that despite the profound impact of a company's strategic logic, that logic is often not articulated. And because it goes unstated and unexamined, a company does not necessarily apply a consistent strategic logic across its businesses.

How can senior executives promote value innovation? First, they must identify and articulate the company's prevailing strategic logic. Then they must challenge it. They must stop and think about the industry's assumptions, the company's strategic focus, and the approaches—to customers, assets and capabilities, and product and service offerings—that are taken as given. Having reframed the company's strategic logic around value innovation, senior executives must ask the four questions that translate that thinking into a new value curve: Which of the factors that our industry takes for granted should be eliminated? Which factors should be reduced well below the industry's standard? Which should be raised well above the industry's standard? What factors should be created that the industry has never offered? Asking the full set of questions—rather than singling out one or two—is necessary for profitable growth. Value innovation is the simultaneous pursuit of radically superior value for buyers and lower costs for companies.

For managers of diversified corporations, the logic of value innovation can be used to identify the most promising possibilities for growth across a portfolio of businesses. The value innovators we studied all have been pioneers in their industries, not necessarily in developing new technologies but in pushing the value they offer customers to new frontiers. Extending the pioneer metaphor can provide a useful way of talking about the growth potential of current and future businesses.

A company's *pioneers* are the businesses that offer unprecedented value. They are the most powerful sources of profitable growth. At the other extreme are *settlers*—businesses with value curves that conform to the basic shape of the industry's. Settlers will not generally contribute much to a company's growth. The potential of *migrators* lies somewhere in between. Such businesses extend the industry's curve by giving customers more for less, but they don't alter its basic shape.

A useful exercise for a management team pursuing growth is to plot the company's current and planned portfolios on a pioneer-migrator-settler map. (See the chart "Testing the Growth Potential of a Portfolio of Businesses.") If both the current portfolio and the planned offerings consist mainly of settlers, the company has a low growth trajectory and needs to push for value innovation. The company may well have fallen into the trap of competing. If current and planned offerings consist of a lot of migrators, reasonable growth can be expected. But the company is not exploiting its potential for growth and risks being marginalized by a value innovator. This exercise is especially valuable for managers who want to see beyond today's performance numbers. Revenue, profitability, market share, and customer satisfaction are all measures of a company's current position. Contrary to what conventional strategic thinking suggests, those measures cannot point the way to the future. The pioneer-migrator-settler map can help a company predict and plan future growth and profit, a task that is especially difficult—and crucial—in a fast-changing economy.

Testing the Growth Potential of a Portfolio of Businesses

The Pioneer-Migrator-Settler Map

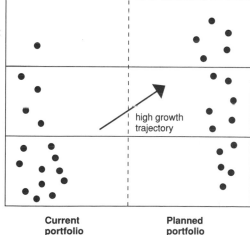

Pioneers
Businesses that represent value innovations

Migrators
Businesses with value improvements

high growth trajectory

Settlers
Businesses that offer me-too products and services

Current portfolio

Planned portfolio

Researching the Roots of High Growth

OVER THE LAST FIVE YEARS, we studied more than 30 companies around the world in approximately 30 industries. We looked at companies with high growth in both revenues and profits and companies with less successful performance records. In an effort to explain the difference in performance between the two groups of companies, we interviewed hundreds of managers, analysts, and researchers. We built strategic, organizational, and performance profiles. We looked for industry or organizational patterns. And we compared the two groups of companies along dimensions that are often thought to be related to a company's potential for growth. Did private companies grow more quickly than public ones? What was the impact on companies of the overall growth of their industry? Did entrepreneurial start-ups have an edge over established incumbents? Were companies led by creative, young radicals likely to grow faster than those run by older managers?

We found that none of those factors mattered in a systematic way. High growth was achieved by both small and large organizations, by companies in high-tech and low-tech industries, by new entrants and incumbents, by private and public companies, and by companies from various countries.

What did matter—consistently—was the way managers in the two groups of companies thought about strategy. In interviewing the managers, we asked them to describe their strategic moves and the thinking behind them. Thus we came to understand their views on each of the five textbook dimensions of strategy: industry assumptions, strategic focus, customers, assets and capabilities, and product and service offerings. We were struck by what emerged from our content analysis of those interviews. The managers of the high-growth companies—irrespective of their industry—all described what we have come to call the logic of value innovation. The managers of the less successful companies all thought along conventional strategic lines.

Intrigued by that finding, we went on to test whether the managers of the high-growth companies applied their strategic thinking to business initiatives in the marketplace. We found that they did.

Furthermore, in studying the business launches of about 100 companies, we were able to quantify the impact of value innovation on a company's growth in both revenues and profits. Although 86% of the launches were line extensions—that is, incremental improvements— they accounted for 62% of total revenues and only 39% of total profits. The remaining 14% of the launches—the true value innovations—generated 38% of total revenues and a whopping 61% of total profits.

Virgin Atlantic: Flying in the Face of Conventional Logic

WHEN VIRGIN ATLANTIC AIRWAYS challenged its indus- try's conventional logic by eliminating first-class service in 1984, the airline was simply following the logic of value innovation. Most of the industry's profitable revenue came from business class, not first class. And first class was a big cost generator. Virgin spotted an opportunity. The airline decided to channel the cost it would save by cutting first-class service into value innovation for business-class passengers.

First, Virgin introduced large, reclining sleeper seats, raising seat comfort in business class well above the industry's standard. Second, Virgin offered free transportation to and from the airport—initially in chauffeured limousines and later in specially designed motorcycles called LimoBikes—to speed business-class passengers through snarled city traffic.

With those innovations, which were on the product and service platforms, Virgin attracted not only a large share of the industry's business-class customers but also some full-economy-fare and first-class passengers of other airlines. Virgin's value innovation separated the company from the pack for many years, but the competition did not stand still. As the value curves of some other airlines began converging with Virgin's value curve, the company went for another leap in value, this time from the service platform.

Virgin observed that most business-class passengers want to use their time productively before and between flights and that, after long-haul flights, they want to freshen up and change their wrinkled clothes before going to meetings. The airline designed lounges where passengers can have their clothes pressed, take showers, enjoy massages, and use state-of-the-art office equipment. The service allows busy executives to make good use of their time and go directly to meetings without first stopping at their hotels—a tremendous value for customers that generates high volume for Virgin. The airline has one of the highest sales per employee in the industry, and its costs per passenger mile are among the lowest. The economics of value innovation create a positive and reinforcing cycle.

When Virgin first challenged the industry's assumptions, its ideas were met with a great deal of skepticism. After all, conventional wisdom says that in order to grow, a company must embrace *more*, not fewer, market segments. But Virgin deliberately walked away from the revenue generated by first-class passengers. And it further violated conventional wisdom by conceiving of its business in terms of customer solutions, even if that took the company well beyond an airline's traditional offerings. Virgin has applied the logic of value innovation not just to the airline industry but also to insurance and to music and entertainment retailing. Virgin has always done more than leverage its existing assets and capabilities. The company has been a consistent value innovator.

Originally published in January–February 1997
Reprint 97108

Growth Through Acquisitions

A Fresh Look

PATRICIA L. ANSLINGER AND
THOMAS E. COPELAND

Executive Summary

MANY COMPANIES TODAY find themselves with a surplus of cash and a shortage of places to use it. In the past five years, more than 1,300 companies have stashed upwards of $150 billion into their coffers. Yet when CEOs look for ways to spend that cash, they find few options. The common wisdom they hear is constricting: Don't reinvest if your industry has low return prospects. Don't pay dividends, because they are double-taxed. Don't pay down debt, because you sacrifice a tax-advantaged source of funds. Don't repurchase shares, because you are shrinking the company. And if you do decide to acquire, make the acquisitions small and synergistic.

This litany, however, precludes one important option—nonsynergistic acquisitions. A new study by McKinsey consultants Patricia L. Anslinger and Thomas E.

Copeland has found that companies can pursue nonsynergistic deals profitably. In fact, their yearlong research has uncovered a diverse group of organizations, including Thermo Electron, Sara Lee, and Clayton, Dubilier & Rice, that have grown dramatically and captured sustained returns of 18% to 35% per year by making nonsynergistic acquisitions.

But making these acquisitions work is not easy. It forces senior managers to ask themselves a difficult set of questions: Are we prepared to change the business of newly acquired companies radically? Should we bring new managers in after the acquisition? How will managers be compensated? Can we have a daily dialogue with senior executives while still allowing them to make operating decisions on their own? Can we make all the necessary changes happen in two years?

THE COMMON WISDOM ON SUCCESSFUL CORPO-RATE ACQUISITIONS IS SHORT AND SIMPLE: Make them small and make them synergistic. Yet companies that rely solely on this view risk missing an entire world of valuable strategic opportunities. Our yearlong research program has shown that companies can pursue a nonsynergistic strategy profitably. In fact, our research has uncovered a diverse group of organizations, including Thermo Electron Corporation, Sara Lee Corporation, and Clayton, Dubilier & Rice, that have grown dramatically and captured sustained returns of 18% to 35% per year by making nonsynergistic acquisitions. (See "Finding Nonsynergistic Acquirers," on page 73.)

Our 21 successful acquirers fell into two groups: diversified public corporate acquirers and financial buyers such as leveraged buyout firms. We chose to study LBO firms because, like the rest of the world, we were fascinated as we watched them outbid corporate buyers and then produce extraordinary returns without the benefit of synergies among their businesses. We compared the LBO firms' practices with those of successful diversified corporate acquirers and were surprised to find that their operating principles were remarkably similar.

Yet many corporate strategists refuse to believe that they can be successful in pursuing nonsynergistic deals. In our view, their hesitancy results from fundamental misconceptions about the way today's nonsynergistic acquirers operate. The first is that financial buyers rely on market timing to buy assets at a low price (turning around and selling them at a high price). In fact, we found that financial buyers actually pay substantial premiums above market price, just as other acquirers do.

The second misconception is that high financial leverage is used to discipline managers. In fact, financial buyers in our study, to avoid losing flexibility, make a conscious effort to prevent high leverage from controlling managers' decision making about operations. Although many LBO firms start out with fairly high debt loads, they reduce their burden to relatively conventional levels (65% debt to total assets) within one to three years. Our findings are supported by the research of John Kitching, who studied 110 buyouts ("Early Returns on LBOs," HBR November–December 1989). He found that by the second year after acquisition, debt repayment of the typical LBO exceeded repayment commitments by 600%.

Without a doubt, the 21 companies in our sample were very successful. Altogether they made 829 acquisitions. When asked whether they earned their cost of capital, 80% of the respondents (accounting for 611 acquisitions) said yes. Our sample of U.S. corporate acquirers averaged more than 18% per year in total return to shareholders over a ten-year period, and the financial acquirers averaged 35% per year by their own estimates.

Although the acquisitions of any given acquirer in our study were seemingly unrelated, successful acquirers picked a common theme and stuck to it. For example, we noted that Clayton, Dubilier & Rice—a financial buyer—was skilled at turnarounds, often shrinking the acquired company before growing it. (See W. Carl Kester and Timothy A. Luehrman, "Rehabilitating the Leveraged Buyout," HBR May–June 1995.) Desai Capital Management, also an LBO firm, searched for growth opportunities in retail-related industries. Emerson Electric Company acquired companies with a core competence in component manufacturing, particularly those for which it could exploit cost-control capabilities. And Sara Lee, which has acquired more than 60 different consumer-product companies—including Coach Leatherware Company, Playtex Apparel, and Champion Products Inc.—used branding and retailing as its common thread.

Using branding and retailing as its common thread, Sara Lee has acquired more than 60 different consumer-product companies.

Making Acquisitions Work

But making this type of acquisition work is not easy. Our research has found that successful corporate and financial buyers use seven key operating principles. These principles affect almost every stage of the acquisition process, from the identification of candidates to post-merger management. They are:

- Insist on innovative operating strategies.

- Don't do the deal if you can't find the leader.

- Offer big incentives to top-level executives.

- Link compensation to changes in cash flow.

- Push the pace of change.

- Foster dynamic relationships among owners, managers, and the board.

- Hire the best acquirers.

Insist on innovative operating strategies. Since the early 1980s, high-profile leveraged buyouts such as Duracell International, Uniroyal, and RJR Nabisco have attracted widespread attention. Much of the fanfare has focused on negotiation tactics, savvy financial structures, and prices. Little attention, however, has been given to the other 2,200-plus buyouts that have occurred in that time period and to the fundamental changes in operating practices that have generated positive returns for many of those companies.[1] Although many observers believe that LBO firms uncover hidden gems in the marketplace, more often they merely focus on improving operations.

Sunglass Hut International and Snapple Beverage Corporation, two acquisitions from our sample group, illustrate that the largest source of value creation in successful acquisitions comes from operating performance, not from financial leverage, market timing, or industry selection.[2] When Desai Capital acquired Sunglass Hut, it concentrated on growing revenues rapidly and created a new strategy to do so. Since the initial acquisition in 1988, Sunglass Hut has grown from 150 stores to more than 800 and has racked up an impressive 37% in annual returns by acquiring, in its turn, smaller stores and implementing a new store format. The company replaced clerks who knew little about sunglasses with trained customer-service specialists, introduced an extensive product assortment instead of relying on two or three popular lines, and instituted a low-price regional strategy. (See the chart "Sources of Value Creation in an Acquisition.")

The Snapple buyout, done by the well-known financial buyer Thomas H. Lee Company in 1992, provides another example of operating innovations. Shortly after the buyout, Snapple embarked on an ambitious growth

Sources of Value Creation in an Acquisition

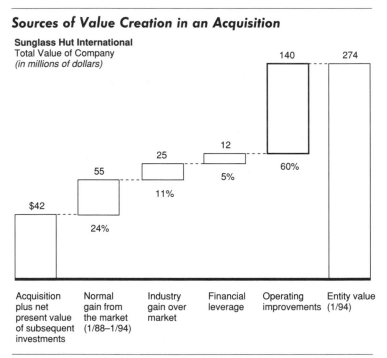

Sunglass Hut International
Total Value of Company
(in millions of dollars)

| Acquisition plus net present value of subsequent investments | Normal gain from the market (1/88–1/94) | Industry gain over market | Financial leverage | Operating improvements | Entity value (1/94) |

$42 — 24% — 55 — 11% — 25 — 5% — 12 — 60% — 140 — 274

Sources: *Private files, McKinsey analysis, Compustat.*

strategy based on rapid geographic expansion and product-line extensions. Knowing that competitors would soon bring out their

Nearly 85% of the respondents in our interviews retained preacquisition managers to run their acquired companies.

own natural teas and fruit juices, the company quickly built its production and distribution system. It established contractual relationships with bottling and distribution companies that had spare production capacity, thereby getting its product to market one year ahead of national competitors such as Fruitopia (from Coca-Cola Company's Minute Maid division) and gaining a first-mover advantage.

As the Snapple example illustrates, innovative operating strategies allow acquirers to be successful in industries as notoriously competitive as the U.S. food and beverage industry. The lesson: Don't look for growth only in high-growth industries.

Don't do the deal if you can't find the leader. More than 65% of our respondents believe that managerial talent is the single most important instrument for creating value. Acquirers ensure that they have the right managers in three ways: They evaluate current executives; they look for managers within the organization who are not yet in leadership positions; they hire outside industry experts.

Nearly 85% of the responding acquirers in our interviews kept preacquisition managers in their positions. In other instances, successful acquirers have found leaders elsewhere in the company—leaders who had not yet had the chance to carry out their vision. Forstmann Little & Company discovered top leaders within middle management at General Instrument, and those individuals have gone on to create more than $3 billion in value over the past three years.

When successful acquirers look for outside industry experts, they tend to find outstanding performers at large corporations. For instance, Stephen Rabinowitz, who had an impressive track record as president of General Electric Lighting and later as vice president of AlliedSignal Braking Systems, was hired to turn General Cable Corporation around in 1994 after Wassall acquired it. Many potential buyers had looked at General Cable, a supplier of copper wire cables, but few knew how to make it profitable. In acquiring General Cable, Wassall was betting that the company could be turned around and that Rabinowitz was the man to do it. Within 18 months of the acquisition, the bet paid off: Rabinowitz had overhauled the company's varied information systems, cut more than 30% of its product offerings, and dramatically reduced working capital.

However, when financial targets are not met, successful acquirers don't hesitate to replace managers. Financial buyers show less patience than corporate acquirers. In 32% of the acquisitions by financial buyers in our study, one or more top-level managers were replaced within three years. In the corporate acquisitions, less than 10% of managers were replaced within three years. Why the difference between corporate and financial buyers? It may be attributable to the taller hurdles imposed by financial buyers or to corporate acquirers' reluctance to displace managers and disrupt a company's culture.

Those reluctant to replace managers might take a lesson from Thomas H. Lee. The company engineered a management buyout of Diet Center in 1988. "We knew management was weak, but we thought we could fix it," recounts former managing director Steven Segal, now managing director of J.W. Childs Associates. At the time of the Diet Center acquisition, Jenny Craig was predominantly an Australian food company and Nutri-System was just emerging from bankruptcy. Neither was a serious threat to Diet Center at first, but both became major competitors before long. When the competition got rough, Diet Center's managers faltered.

Offer big incentives to top-level executives. Finding and motivating the right managers is so important that many successful acquirers offer senior executives significant ownership stakes (usually 10% to 20%). If all goes as planned, those managers can become millionaires. Why offer such big carrots? B. Charles Ames, a Clayton, Dubilier & Rice partner, said it best, "Managers are more committed to doing the difficult work of restructuring, growing, and otherwise fixing an acquisition when some or all of their net worth is on the line." Creating annual returns in excess of 35%, as these managers must, requires a great deal of commitment and effort.

Incentives are especially important when new managers are recruited into a company. In that case, substantial upside potential is often needed to woo outstanding executives away from comfortable and relatively low-risk jobs. Previous studies on buyouts have shown that CEOs of acquired companies typically hold 6.4% of their unit's equity, whereas the average CEO of a public company might hold only .25%.[3]

Some managers must put a large part of their net worth at risk. This is called "pain equity."

In most of the cases we studied, executives are obliged to purchase enough stock so that their holdings constitute a large part of their net worth. These large holdings are often referred to as "pain equity"—a way to ensure that managers cannot afford to fail. If an executive is unable to buy the equity, acquirers may offer a discount or a loan.

A major controversy has erupted over whether public companies should follow these practices. Some argue that public companies cannot offer large ownership stakes to individual managers because shareholders monitor executive pay to ensure that it is "reasonable." However, the best acquirers in our study, such as Thermo Electron Corporation, aren't afraid to make top managers wealthy if their companies achieve outstanding returns. In fact, almost 60% of our corporate acquirers offer managers a chance to become much wealthier than their industry peers. Thermo Electron alone has created 40 millionaires. However, such acquirers are shrewd and give up only as much equity as required to lure the best talent.

Equity stakes are not the only motivating factor for managers, of course. Other forms of reward, such as public recognition and future advancement (within large corporate parents), are also needed to make the difficulties and uncertainty worthwhile to managers. Nonmonetary forms of compensation are particularly prevalent at public corporations, where executives with the best performance records are rewarded in a variety of ways.

Link compensation to changes in cash flow. Besides issuing equity up front, successful acquirers motivate executives with carefully designed compensation schemes tied to changes in cash flow. Such incentive pay accomplishes two objectives. First, it's a reward for current efforts—a symbol of recognition, a pat on the back. Second and more important, it provides a foundation—a common vocabulary—for communication between managers and owners so that managers will keep cash flow in mind when making daily operating decisions.

Many of the acquirers we studied pay managers a base salary set at roughly the average for the industry. However, they tie a substantial amount of total compensation to annual performance measures. They evaluate which measures are the most important drivers of operating cash flow and then set aggressive targets. Factors that affect current cash flow, such as inventory on hand, accounts receivable, and unit growth, are generally used along with variables that affect longer-term cash flows, such as return on new capital investment and gains in market share. These metrics are derived from overall business targets and are often incorporated into senior managers' employment contracts, with explicit numerical targets set for each variable. Bonus payouts usually range from 50% to 100% or more of base salary. The size of the reward is correlated closely with the difficulty of achieving specific performance goals.

In 1993, when Kirkland Messina, a buyout firm in Los Angeles, acquired the Selmer Company, a maker of musical instruments, it knew it had to resolve a severe lack of communication among Selmer's departments. It discovered, for example, that the sales force was not properly informing the manufacturing group of its inventory needs. The confusion caused the company to miss critical delivery dates on its highest-margin products: trumpets for professional musicians.

"The company was run in fiefdoms," says CEO Dana Messina. Kirkland Messina changed all that: "We set up measures that forced partnering between functional areas. Sales managers have margin as well as revenue targets; manufacturing managers have customer-delivery

as well as working-capital targets." The result: Managers'
cash compensation has doubled, and cash flow has
increased 50% in the two years since the acquisition.

Push the pace of change. "When it comes to identifying opportunities, time is critical," says Charlie Peters,
vice president of development and technology at Emerson Electric. "Most of the actions required to create
value are taken in the first two years after the deal is
closed." Both public and private acquirers agree that
pushing the pace of change disciplines managers and
sharpens priorities. It gives people in the organization a
sense of urgency and a challenge. For example, Emerson
acquired Fisher Controls International, a supplier of
manufacturing process control equipment, in late 1992.
Because of a series of operating changes—including
plant consolidations, changes in procurement practices,
inventory programs, and sales-force alignments—both
profit and cash flows were able not only to meet aggressive two-year plans but also to exceed the original acquisition forecast. Emerson is not alone; Grand Metropolitan also makes change happen fast. After acquiring PET
in February 1995, the company quickly moved to close
plants, reduce costs at headquarters, and change brand
strategy.

At WESCO, a buyout done by Clayton, Dubilier &
Rice, operating income jumped from almost no profits
to profits of roughly $55 million within two years. The
previous owner, Westinghouse Electric Corporation, had
sought to maximize profits by keeping manufacturing
utilization high—a strategy that meant WESCO sometimes sold products at a loss. Following the acquisition,
the new management team announced that the company was no longer in business to sell the maximum

amount of product; it designed a new sales-incentive plan that rewarded the sales force for boosting gross margins instead of focusing on volume. Procurement and inventory control were improved by charging the branch managers 1% per month for inventory held less than two months and 2% for inventory held more than two months.

Foster dynamic relationships among owners, managers, and the board. One critical difference between successful acquirers and most corporations is the level of interaction among managers, directors, and shareholders. Rather than erect a multitier, bureaucratic structure, successful acquirers create flat organizations. Sara Lee, for instance, employs a decentralized management structure that divides the corporation into discrete profit centers, each led by an executive with a high degree of authority and accountability for the performance of that business.

Other successful acquirers keep acquired businesses separate from other operating units, even if that policy precludes exploitation of potential synergies. They believe that giving acquired businesses a high degree of autonomy is essential.

The way Thermo Electron is organized illustrates the point. In the past ten years, Thermo Electron has acquired 30 companies in the environmental, energy, health care, and medical equipment industries. It owns between 50% and 80% of the stock of its operating units; the remainder is in the hands of the public. By structuring his company in this manner, CEO George Hatsopoulos has been able to offer a large and diverse group of managers equity stakes; yet he has maintained control by having key officers report to Thermo

Electron and by having formal contractual agreements
that specify operating policy. For example, each operating company is required to put its funds into a centralized cash-management sys-

*Thermo Electron's
operating units have the
independence of public
companies with the
reporting relationships
of subsidiaries.*

tem controlled by Thermo
Electron, to follow internal
control and accounting
procedures, to submit
annual and five-year plans,
and to report to Thermo
Electron's senior executives
about deviations from plan. In short, the operating
units have the independence of public companies with
the control and reporting relationships that are common in corporate subsidiaries.

More than 80% of the successful acquirers studied
allow top-level managers to have the final say in all operational decisions as long as financial targets are met.
The rest make major operational decisions jointly.
Financial buyers in particular rarely override the decisions of upper management, in spite of having controlling equity positions. As a representative of one stated,
"We have the same power as corporate parents, but we
are less willing to use it."

The best financial and corporate buyers often appoint
a gatekeeper to be the interface between owner and
operating unit manager. That individual becomes inti-
mately involved in the acquired company's operating
decisions by acting as a sounding board for management, especially during the first 6 to 18 months after the
acquisition. "We talk daily [with the CEO] for the first
few months, until major change has happened; then we
talk weekly," says Thomas Weld, a managing director of
Three Cities Research, a financial buyer.

Successful acquirers also carefully structure the boards of directors of acquired companies, limiting them to five to seven members. The boards typically consist of one to three managers from the acquired company, one or two industry experts, and two or three representatives from the ownership group. Financial buyers generally use outsiders on their boards to provide an independent point of view. In the case of corporate acquirers, however, industry experts are usually the CEOs of other operating units in related lines of business; owners are typically represented by the group head or holding company president. Both corporate and financial acquirers prefer a majority of seats on the board to be held by equity owners (managers and investors).

Hire the best acquirers. One often overlooked aspect of acquisitions is selecting the deal makers. These individuals make judgments that are often critical to the success or failure of the transaction. Here the differences between financial buyers and corporate acquirers may lead to some differences in value creation.

Financial buyers hire highly skilled professionals with outstanding professional and educational credentials. In our sample of nine buyout firms and more than 100 professionals, 45% of professionals had previous experience making deals at either an investment bank or some other major investing firm. Another 35% had top-level operating or consulting experience. The educational background of investment professionals also suggests that they are drawn from an elite pool. More than 75% of associates and partners studied had advanced degrees in business or law, and more than 90% of those degrees came from high-ranked U.S. schools.

The best and the brightest don't come cheap. Starting compensation for associates can be greater than $100,000 per year and can grow to more than $500,000 within five years. The opportunity for associates to influence the actions of managers at acquired companies also gives them a powerful nonmonetary motivator: a strong sense of impact. At a more senior level, the financial rewards are huge. Partners at successful firms usually earn in excess of $1 million per year from a combination of management fees, incentive ("override") payments from realized investments, as well as capital appreciation of stock.

Corporate acquirers pursue a different strategy for building their acquisition teams. Unlike financial buyers, they tend to hire people with less deal-making experience, preferring to develop their own talent. Corporate investment professionals generally possess fewer advanced degrees and come from less prestigious schools. They are paid significantly less than their counterparts at financial firms. Unlike financial buyers, where both senior and junior staff evaluate the desirability of an acquisition, corporate buyers typically have senior executives make those decisions. Staff associates are limited to structuring the deal, negotiating it, and working out legal and accounting issues. The prospect of fast-track promotion serves as the key motivator for corporate investment professionals, rather than the decision-making autonomy and financial rewards offered by financial buyers. Do corporate acquirers lose anything by not hiring the same type of people as financial buyers do? Although this hypothesis cannot be tested directly, our analysis of the two groups' respective acquisition processes and returns suggests that they do.

How to Do It

Many companies today find themselves with a surplus of cash and a shortage of places to use it profitably. In the past five years, more than 1,300 companies have collectively stashed $150 billion in their coffers.

We believe that most companies can benefit from the nonsynergistic approach to acquisitions we have described. However, cash-rich companies should consider carefully the magnitude of change that will be required. Taking into account their company's skills, organizational structure, and corporate culture, they should do one of the following to implement the strategy.

Our respondents found that they did not have to stay in their core businesses but could grow within their field of knowledge.

Evolve in-house capabilities. This approach is most suited to those companies that already have the right frame of mind—those that are entrepreneurial and growth oriented and that already follow many of our key operating principles. Most likely such companies are currently running highly autonomous operating units, sometimes with separate legal structures, albeit with close ties to the parent corporation. Here most changes will be evolutionary rather than revolutionary and will be geared to bringing acquisition and management techniques in line with best practices.

Companies thinking of developing in-house acquisition capabilities will need to screen potential acquisitions, structure sophisticated deals, and monitor portfolio companies effectively. In addition, they will need to develop individualized performance-based evaluation and compensation systems. Specifically, we recommend that headquarters allow each subsidiary to pursue its own long-range strategy, have a separate management compensation plan, and pursue acquisitions in its main line of business. Nonsynergistic acquisitions and spin-offs, however, should be managed by the parent company, as should selection and removal of high-level subsidiary managers.

Establish a separate subsidiary. Where a company's business system and culture are likely to reject nonconforming additions, we recommend creating an acquisition group outside the core organization. Many multi-business or single operating companies, especially those that are highly centralized or have strong corporate cultures, would find this approach the most appropriate for them. Companies that wish to copy the operating practices of successful acquirers must be confident that they have or can find the skills necessary to run an independent acquisition program within the guidelines suggested here. At various times, some public companies, including General Electric Company and Hanson Trust, have set up or spun off operations to allow for the autonomy and flexibility needed to invest in businesses outside their core businesses. At Chemical Bank, Chemical Venture Partners was established as an autonomously managed partnership, yet the bank is the only limited partner and the employees are Chemical Bank employees.

Outsource. A company without an experienced team of advisers can hire outside assistance. However, the advisers' interests must align with the company's. If a company uses investment bankers, for example, it must realize that the way deal fees are structured makes completing a transaction the highest priority of such advisers. The risk: overpayment on price, hurried due diligence, overly simplistic contracts, and little premerger planning.

Another option exists for those whose corporate climate is suited to partnerships. A company wishing to make nonsynergistic acquisitions can benefit from a partnership with a financial buyer experienced in nonsynergistic deals. For example, Oak Industries, a manufacturer of consumer components, formed a successful partnership with Bain Capital in 1992 to acquire Gilbert Engineering, a specialty-connector manufacturer for cable television.

Any CEO who wants to implement our guidelines in his or her own company must ask, Am I confident that I can buy into new businesses and generate maximum returns from my investment dollars? Ultimately, for a company to become a successful acquirer, executives must think in ways that are unorthodox and uncomfortable to them. Each of the successful acquirers in our study made purchases where others failed to discern a path to success. Yet the acquirers in our survey did succeed in exporting their knowledge to new businesses. Thus, interpreted properly, "Stick to your knitting" does not mean a company should stay in its core business. It really means a company should grow within its field of knowledge. Our sample of acquirers did just that.

Finding Nonsynergistic Acquirers

TO FIND THE MOST SUCCESSFUL NONSYNERGISTIC ACQUIRERS, we screened all major companies making acquisitions over the past ten years—U.S. and U.K. public companies and known U.S. financial buyers. In selecting

U.S. and U.K. Public Corporate Acquirers, 1985–1994

Companies	1994 Sales (in millions of dollars)	Annualized Return	Number of Acquisitions and Divestitures	Degree of Diversification
Index: S&P 500		14.3		
Berkshire Hathaway	3,847.5	32.0%	26	16
Phelps Dodge Corporation	3,289.0	29.7	10+	4
Sara Lee Corporation	15,536.0	23.7	85	9
Thermo Electron Corporation	1,585.3	22.4	30	12
Illinois Tool Works	3,461.3	21.8	10	5
Canagra	23,512.2	20.4	95+	8
Alco Standard Corporation	7,992.5	18.3	62	9
Air Products and Chemicals	3,485.3	17.2	10	5
General Electric Company	59,316.0	17.2	76	24
Dover Corporation	3,085.3	14.3	11	5
Emerson Electric Company*	8,607.2	13.9	40	4
Harcourt General*	3,208.5	13.1	10	4
MSCI Index (U.K.)		5.4		
Wassal	1,022.0	14.4	11	5
Bat Industries	28,169.3	14.1	10	7
Hanson Trust	16,899.7	9.8	31	20
Grand Metropolitan	11,740.3	7.6	47	9

*Although they did not exceed the total return of the S&P 500 Index over the ten-year time frame, these companies experienced periods of excellence between 1980 and 1994.

Sources: Annual reports, company interviews, Compustat, Securities Data Corporation.

public corporations, we chose those that had acquired more than ten companies of size that were in more than four different major lines of business. Since some companies acquire a variety of businesses in order to vertically integrate, we saw them as one business and therefore eliminated them from our sample. (See the table "U.S. and U.K. Public Corporate Acquirers, 1985-1994.")

For financial buyers, we chose firms that had disclosed investment funds of $250 million or more and that had raised at least two investment funds—an indicator of successful investment performance over time. (See the table "Financial Buyers.")

We then conducted detailed interviews with eight corporate acquirers and 13 financial buyers. The group of

Financial Buyers

Firm	Size of Capital (in millions of dollars)	Number of Funds Raised
Kohlberg, Kravis, Roberts & Company	9,200	3
Morgan Stanley Capital Partners	4,281	6
E.M. Warburg, Pincus & Company	3,675	2
Clayton, Dubilier & Rice	2,985	5
Stonington Partners	2,900	3
Thomas H. Lee Company	2,721	3
Hellman & Friedman	2,704	3
Chemical Venture Partners	2,500	
GS Capital Venture Partners	2,500	2
The Blackstone Group	2,081	2
Acadia Partners/Oak Hill Partners	1,800	5
Forstmann Little & Company	1,582	5
Apollo Advisors	1,500	3

Financial Buyers *(continued)*

Firm	Size of Capital *(in millions of dollars)*	Number of Funds Raised
Kelso & Company	1,335	5
Freeman, Spogil & Company	1,130	3
Boston Ventures Management	1,042	4
Hicks, Muse, Tate & Furst	1,032	3
TA Associates	800	7
Desai Capital Management	675	3
Joseph, Littlejohn & Levy	620	2
Carlyle Group	600	2
Three Cities Research	600	3
Gibbons, Goodwin, Van Amerongen	560	3
Charterhouse Group International	556	2
Welsh, Carson, Anderson & Stowe IV	552	5
Golder, Thoma, Cressey, Rauner	547	7
Leonard Green & Partners	535	2
Dillon, Read & Company/ Saratoga Partners	513	3
American Industrial Partners Management Company	495	2
Bain Capital	445	7
Castle, Harlan	379	3
McCown, DeLeeuw & Company	340	3
Aurora Capital Partners	320	2
GE Investments	309	2
Berkshire Partners	295	3
Morgan, Lewis, Githen & Ahn	285	
Weiss, Peck & Greer	275	7

Sources: Asset Alternatives *and* Corporate Finance *(Winter 1994)*.

corporate acquirers in the study operated 50 different lines of business, outperformed the Standard & Poor 500 and Morgan Stanley Capital International (MSCI) indices by an average of almost 50%, and experienced compound annual revenue growth of 12% during the past ten years. The group of financial buyers in the study had reported capital of more than $16 billion and achieved estimated returns above 25% annually for their funds, with many producing returns exceeding 40%. If these financial buyers were viewed as corporate conglomerates, their 1994 revenues would place 45% of them in the *Fortune* 500.

Notes

1. William F. Long and David J. Ravenscraft, "Decade of Debt: Lessons from LBOs in the 1980s." In *The Deal Decade: What Takeovers and Leveraged Buyouts Mean for Corporate Governance*, ed. Margaret M. Blair (Washington, D.C.: Brookings Institution, 1993).

2. Various academic studies of LBOs support our findings that successful diverse acquirers are able to create value mainly by improving operations. See Steven Kaplan, "The Effects of Management Buyouts on Operating Performance and Value," *Journal of Financial Economics* 24 (1989), p. 217.

3. Michael C. Jensen, "Eclipse of the Public Corporation," HBR September–October 1989, p. 61.

Originally published in January–February 1996
Reprint 96101

Bradley Boyer and Kristin Fink, both of McKinsey & Company, helped prepare this article.

To Diversify or Not to Diversify

CONSTANTINOS C. MARKIDES

Executive Summary

ONE OF THE MOST CHALLENGING DECISIONS a company can confront is whether to diversify. The rewards and risks are extraordinary. Success stories such as General Electric, Disney, and 3M abound, but so do stories of failure—consider Quaker Oats' entry into the fruit juice business with Snapple.

What makes diversification such an unpredictable, high-stakes game? First, companies usually face the decision in an atmosphere that is not conducive to thoughtful deliberation. For example, an attractive company comes into play, and a competitor is interested in buying it. Or the board of directors urges expanding into new markets. Suddenly, senior managers must synthesize mountains of data under intense time pressure. To complicate matters, diversification as a corporate strategy regularly goes in and out of vogue. In short, there is little conventional wisdom to guide managers as they consider a move that could greatly increase shareholder value or seriously damage it.

But diversification doesn't need to be quite such a roll of the dice, argues the author. His research suggests that if managers consider six questions, they can reduce the gamble of diversification. Answering the questions will not lead to an easy go-no-go decision, but by helping managers weigh risks and opportunities, it can help them assess the likelihood of success.

The issues that the questions raise, and the discussion they provoke, are meant to be coupled with the detailed financial analysis usually conducted before a diversification decision is made. Together, these tools can turn a complex and often pressured decision into a more structured and well-reasoned one.

ONE OF THE MOST CHALLENGING DECISIONS A COMPANY CAN CONFRONT is whether to diversify: the rewards and risks can be extraordinary. Success stories abound—think of General Electric, Disney, and 3M—but so do stories of such infamous and costly failures as Quaker Oats' entry into (and exit from) the fruit juice business with Snapple, and RCA's forays into computers, carpets, and rental cars.

What makes diversification such an unpredictable, high-stakes game? First, companies usually face the decision in an atmosphere not conducive to thoughtful deliberation. For example, an attractive company comes into play, and a competitor is interested in buying it. Or the board of directors strongly urges expanding into new markets. Suddenly, senior managers must synthesize mountains of data—including internal-rate-of-return calculations, market forecasts, and competitive assessments—under intense time pressure. To complicate matters, diversification as a corporate strategy goes in and out of vogue on a regular basis. In other words, there is little conventional wisdom to guide managers as they consider a move that could greatly increase shareholder value or seriously damage it.

But diversification doesn't need to be quite such a roll of the dice. Yes, it always will involve uncertainty; all major business decisions do. And indeed, there is a wealth of good advice about how to approach diversification.[1] But my research suggests that if managers consider the following six questions, they can push their thinking still further to reduce the gamble of diversification. Answering the questions will not lead to an easy go-no-go decision, but the exercise can help managers assess the likelihood of success.

The issues the questions raise, and the discussion they provoke, are meant to be coupled with the detailed financial analysis typical of the diversification decision-making process. Together, these tools can turn a complex and often pressured decision into a more structured and well-reasoned one.

Thus, when managers consider whether or not to diversify, they should ask themselves the following questions:

What can our company do better than any of its competitors in its current market? Just as it is important to take stock of the pantry before going shopping, so is it crucial for a company to identify its unique

and unassailable competitive strengths before attempting to apply them elsewhere. The first step, then, is to
determine the exact nature of those strengths—which I
refer to in general terms as *strategic assets.*

How is such an assessment usually done? Incom-
pletely, I'm afraid. The problem is that most companies
confuse identifying strategic assets with defining their
business. A business is generally defined by using one of
three frameworks: product, customer function, or core
competencies.[2] Thus, depending on its approach, Sony
could decide that it is in the business of electronics,
entertainment, or "pocket-ability."

When facing the decision to diversify, however, managers need to think not about what their company *does*
but about what it *does better* than its competitors. In
one sense, pinpointing
strategic assets is a mar-
ket-driven approach to
business definition. It
forces an organization
to identify how it might
add value to an acquired
company or in a new market—be it with excellent distribution, creative employees, or superior knowledge about
information transfer. In other words, the decision to
diversify is made not on the basis of a broad or vague
business definition, such as "We're in the entertainment
business." Rather, it is made on the basis of a realistic
identification of strategic assets: "Our excellent distribution capabilities could radically improve the performance of the acquired company."

Consider the case of Blue Circle Industries, a British
company that is one of the world's leading cement producers. In the 1980s, Blue Circle decided to diversify on

*Before diversifying,
managers must think not
about what their company
does but about what it does
better than its competitors.*

the basis of an unclear definition of its business. It was, the company's managers determined, in the business of making products related to home building. So Blue Circle expanded into real estate, bricks, waste management, gas stoves, bathtubs—even lawn mowers. According to one retired executive, "Our move into lawn mowers was based on the logic that you need a lawn mower for your garden—which, after all, is next to your house." Not surprisingly, few of Blue Circle's diversification forays proved successful.

Blue Circle's less focused, business-definition approach to diversification didn't answer the more relevant question: What are our company's strategic assets, and how and where can we make the best use of them?

One company that did ask that question—and reaped the rewards—is the United Kingdom's Boddington Group. In 1989, Boddington's then chairman, Denis Cassidy, assessed the company's competitive situation. At the time, Boddington was a vertically integrated beer producer that owned a brewery, wholesalers, and pubs throughout the country. But consolidation was changing the beer industry, making it hard for small players like Boddington to make a profit. The company had survived up to that point because its main strategic asset was in retailing and hospitality: it excelled at managing pubs. So Cassidy decided to diversify in that direction.

Quickly, the company sold off the brewery and acquired resort hotels, restaurants, nursing homes, and health clubs while keeping its large portfolio of pubs. "The decision to abandon brewing was a painful one, especially because the brewery has been a part of us for more than 200 years," Cassidy says. "But given the changes taking place in the business, we realized we could not play the brewing game with the big boys. We

decided to build on our excellent skills in retailing, hospitality, and property management to start a new game."
Boddington's diversification resulted in the creation of
enormous shareholder value—especially when compared with the strategies adopted by regional brewers
that decided to remain in the business. It also illustrates
what happens when a company moves beyond a
business-definition approach and instead launches a
diversification effort based on its strategic assets.

**What strategic assets do we need in order to suc-
ceed in the new market?** Once a company has identified its strategic assets, it can consider this second question. Although the question seems straightforward
enough, my research suggests that many companies
make a fatal error. They assume that having *some* of the
necessary strategic assets is sufficient to move forward
with diversification. In reality, a company usually must
have *all* of them.

The diversification misadventures of a number of oil
companies in the late 1970s highlight how dangerous it
is to go up against a royal flush when all you have is a
pair of jacks. Companies such as British Petroleum and
Exxon broke into the
mineral business believ-
ing they could exploit
their competencies in
exploration, extraction,
and management of
large-scale projects. Ten years later, the companies had
dropped out of the game. The reason: in addition to the
oil companies' capabilities, the mineral business
required low-cost extraction capabilities and access to
deposits, which the oil companies lacked.

> *To diversify, a company
> must have all the necessary
> strategic assets, not just
> some of them.*

Consider as well the experience of the Coca-Cola Company, long heralded for its intimate knowledge of consumers, its marketing and branding expertise, and its superior distribution capabilities. Based on those strategic assets, Coca-Cola decided in the early 1980s to acquire its way into the wine business, in which such strengths were imperative. The company quickly learned, however, that it lacked a critical competence: knowledge of the wine business. Having 90% of what it took to succeed in the new industry was not enough for Coke, because the 10% it did not have—the ability to make quality wine—was the most critical component of success.

As in poker, the lesson for companies considering diversification is the same: you have to know when to hold them and when to fold them. If a company is holding only a pair of strategic assets in an industry in which most players have a better hand, there's no point in putting money on the table—unless, that is, the next question can be answered in the affirmative.

Can we catch up to or leapfrog competitors at their own game? What if Coke had known in advance that it lacked an important strategic asset in the wine-making business? Should it have summarily abandoned its diversification plans?

Not necessarily. Companies considering diversification need to answer another pair of questions: If we are missing one or more critical factors for success in the new market, can we purchase them, develop them, or make them unnecessary by changing the competitive rules of the industry? Can we do that at a reasonable cost?

Consider the diversification history of Sharp Corporation. In the early 1950s, the company decided to leverage its existing strengths in the manufacturing and retailing of radios by moving first into televisions and then into microwave ovens. Sharp licensed the television technology from RCA and acquired the microwave oven technology by working with Litton, the U.S. innovator in that technology. Similarly, Sharp diversified into the electronic calculator business in the 1960s by buying the necessary technology from Rockwell.

The Walt Disney Company has diversified following a similar strategy, expanding from its core animation business into theme parks, live entertainment, cruise lines, resorts, planned residential communities, TV broadcasting, and retailing by buying or developing the strategic assets it needed along the way. For example, Disney's cross-promotional relationships with McDonald's and Mattel gave it an edge in retailing, and its close working relationship with the Florida state government gave the company the expertise it needed in the theme park business.

We can return to Sharp to illustrate how companies lacking crucial strategic assets can build them in-house. In 1969, Sharp invested $21 million—about one-quarter of the company's equity at the time—to build a large-scale-integrated-circuit factory and a central R&D lab to facilitate entry into the semiconductor business. In the 1990s, it has made even bigger investments in order to bring the company up to speed in the liquid-crystal-display industry. Between 1990 and 1992 alone, Sharp invested $540 million in liquid-crystal-display factories and earmarked an additional $550 million for future investments.

A final option for companies lacking the right strategic assets to play in a new market is to rewrite that market's rules of competition, thereby making the missing assets obsolete. One case in point is Canon, which wanted to diversify from its core business of cameras into photocopiers in the early 1960s. Canon boasted strong competencies in photographic technology and dealer management. But it faced formidable competition from Xerox, which dominated the high-speed-copier market, targeting large businesses through its well-connected direct sales force. In addition, Xerox leased rather than sold its machines—a strategic choice that had worked well for the company in its earlier battles with IBM, Kodak, and 3M.

After studying the industry, Canon decided to play the game differently: The company targeted small and midsize businesses, as well as the consumer market. Then it sold its machines outright through a network of dealers rather than through a direct sales force, and it further differentiated its products from those of Xerox by focusing on quality and price rather than speed. As a result, whereas IBM and Kodak failed to make any significant inroads into photocopiers, Canon emerged as the market leader (in unit sales) within 20 years of entering the business. It was, however, a radically different business because of the way Canon had transformed it.

Not all companies have the skill, financial strength, and managerial foresight to pull off what Canon did. But, together with Sharp and Disney, Canon provides an excellent example for companies considering diversification without all the required strategic assets in hand. Those assets must be obtained one way or another; otherwise, moving forward into new markets is likely to backfire.

Will diversification break up strategic assets that need to be kept together? If managers have cleared the hurdles that the preceding questions raise, they then need to ask whether the strategic assets they intend to export are indeed transportable to the new industry. Too many companies mistakenly assume that they can break up clusters of competencies or skills that, in fact, work only because they are together, reinforcing one another in a particular competitive context. Such a misjudgment can doom a diversification move.

An academic exercise conducted several times with managers attending London Business School's executive education program illustrates precisely how easy it is to fall into the trap of breaking up strategic assets that are best left together.[3] The executives were asked to decide which new business McDonald's should enter: frozen foods, theme parks, or photo processing. Forty percent of the executives suggested that because the company's main competencies were finding good real-estate locations and offering family entertainment, it should enter the theme park business. Thirty percent singled McDonald's out for its management of distribution outlets and its skill in making products of consistent quality, and suggested that the photo-processing business would be an appropriate diversification move. The remaining 30% pointed to competencies in distribution, food retailing, and relationships with suppliers, and concluded that the frozen-food business made the most sense.

Managers need to ask whether their strategic assets are transportable to the industry they have targeted.

Interestingly, few executives voiced concern about the risks of unbundling competencies and applying them in different combinations in new markets. Yet in reality, the success of McDonald's in the fast-food business can be attributed to the synergy that exists between those competencies—which support and reinforce one another—and to the fit between the collection of those competencies and the competitive demands of the fast-food market. Indeed, I find it useful to think of interrelated competencies as organisms living in a symbiotic relationship within a particular environment. You cannot separate them and move them elsewhere and expect them to flourish as usual, just as you cannot take the engine out of an airplane and expect it to fly.

To put it in more practical terms, if a company plans to break apart, recombine, and relocate its strategic assets, it also must be prepared to create a hospitable new environment for them. Consider the story of Swatch, the popular mass-market watch made by the Société Suisse de Microelectronique et d'Horlogerie (SMH).

Until the 1980s, SMH was primarily in the business of selling expensive watches to wealthy individuals through jewelers and specialist distributors. Its primary strategic assets were patented knowledge of ultrathin, precision-movement technology, knowledge of process automation, and a reputation for Swiss quality. That cluster, however, was inadequate for competing in the mass market, which required large-scale distribution, cutting-edge designs, and additional purchasing skills.

To overcome that problem, SMH acquired design skills from scratch by establishing the Swatch Design Lab in Milan, which employs artists, designers, and architects from all over the world. At the same time, it developed the required purchasing skills in-house. To gain better distribution, SMH entered into a joint venture with another company, Bhamco. Finally, it combined its new strategic assets with its existing competence in precision-movement technology.

By now, the whole world knows of Swatch's success as a product, but what happened before it hit the market is perhaps even more impressive. The company's managers knew which strategic assets were necessary, created or bought those that were missing, and then combined them with the existing strategic assets, creating a symbiotic, self-reinforcing organization. The company's move into the mass-market watch business, then, stands as an unusual case of core competencies being recombined for success in a new market.

Will we be simply a player in the new market or will we emerge a winner? Even if companies storm into new markets with all the required competencies—put together in the right combination—they still can fail to gain a foothold. Why? To achieve a sustainable advantage, diversifying companies need to create something unique. A company's competitive advantage will be short-lived, and diversification will fail, if competitors in the new industry can imitate the company's moves quickly and cheaply, purchase the necessary strategic assets in the open market, or find an effective substitute for them. In other words, there is no point rushing into a new market unless you have a way to beat the existing players at their own game.

Take the experience of Japanese consumer-goods giant Kao. Kao's chemical division had developed a technology that enabled the company to alter or smooth the surfaces of products such as clothes and magnetic tapes. In the late 1980s, Kao introduced the technology into its detergent division, where it quickly was a major success, allowing the company to create a new kind of laundry detergent. (The detergent, called Attack, was protected by 91 patents.) Within two years, Kao's market share in the laundry detergent business increased from 30% to 56%.

Hoping to build on that success, Kao then transferred the same technology to its floppy-disk division. The effort was not as successful. Simply put, the technology changed and improved the laundry detergent business, but it was old news in the floppy-disk business: competitors either had something similar to it already or had another technology that did the job. Kao had tried to enter a market with a strategic asset that didn't buy it a competitive advantage. The company could play in the floppy-disk industry, but it couldn't win.

How can managers assess whether their company's strategic assets have a strong likelihood of catapulting it to market leadership? A three-part acid test can help.

First, managers should ask if the strategic assets they intend to introduce into a new market are rare. For example, Laker Airways soared in the packaged-vacation business from 1966 to 1976 on the basis of its low-cost, low-price strategy. But in the mid-1970s, when Laker tried to diversify into the transatlantic scheduled-airline business, it bumped into British Airways and the large U.S.-based airlines, and discovered that its low-cost competencies were not unique. British Airways, for example, used its reservations systems and skills in predicting the volume of passengers on flights to offer similar bargains. Laker went bankrupt in 1982.

Second, managers should ask, Can the strategic asset be imitated? 3M, for example, continues to diversify profitably on the strength of a competence that is very hard to copy: an organizational culture that fosters creativity, innovation, and entrepreneurship. Despite the numerous companies paying lip service to those ideals, very few can build and sustain success in the way 3M has.

Third, managers need to ask whether the strategic asset they plan to export can be substituted. Even if competitors can't copy a strategic asset, they may be able to create something similar enough that duplication doesn't matter. Dell Computer was able to substitute IBM's dealers and sales force by selling directly to the consumer. First Direct bank was able to substitute Barclay's extensive branch network in the British banking industry by reaching customers over the phone. In contrast, try as they might, Pepsi and other soft-drink makers cannot replicate or substitute Coca-Cola's strong brand name; hence the company's apparently unassailable competitive edge.

Of course, no company will intentionally diversify into an industry in which it will lose money. But managers considering a new market venture must decide how much money they want to make. For shareholders, being a contender is not enough. They seek winners, and winning is about unique and competitively meaningful strategic assets.

What can our company learn by diversifying, and are we sufficiently organized to learn it? Forward-thinking managers not only will be concerned with success in new markets, but, like good chess players, also will be thinking two or three moves ahead. They will ask themselves a final question when considering a diversification move: What will we learn by entering a new business, and will it serve as a strategic stepping-stone to help us enter yet other businesses? Often, companies can use what they have learned from one diversification move to enter a third market more quickly and cheaply. For example, by diversifying into the copier business, Canon learned how to build a marketing organization targeted to business customers and how to develop and manufacture a reliable

Like good chess players, forward-thinking managers will think two or three moves ahead.

electrostatic-printing engine. As a result, when Canon diversified into the laser printer business—which required the same competencies—it was able to move with speed and ease.

Managers also should examine whether a diversification move will allow them to learn competencies that can be reapplied in their existing businesses. For example, when Canon entered the laser printer business, it developed the capabilities required to support the design, manufacture, and service of sophisticated electronics. The company then took this knowledge and applied it to its photocopier business, vastly improving the electronic controls that allow its machines to count copies and sense paper jams.

Last, managers should ask themselves if their organization is doing all it can to transfer relevant information and competencies from one line of business to another. For such a flow to take place, companies need to have processes that facilitate and promote learning across different functions and divisions. An excellent example of this dynamic at work is Denmark's Lan & Spar Bank. CEO Peter Schou explains that the bank's key diversification moves—such as its recent entry into the direct-banking business—have been supported and fully harvested because 17 employee working groups from throughout the organization meet regularly to share new business ideas and information. In addition, certain people in the company are continually transferred from one area to another to act as "integrators" and "messengers" of new information. By moving knowledge around inside the company in this way, Lan & Spar has taken full advantage of diversification. Indeed, even though the company ranks fortieth in Denmark in terms of the size of deposits, it has ranked number one in industry profitability in five of the last seven years.

THE LESSONS THAT CAN BE LEARNED FROM A COMPANY'S DIVERSIFICATION MOVES CAN BE SIGNIFICANT, but, as we have seen, there are five other important questions for managers to ask before taking the leap into a new market. Those questions should help managers walk the fine line between being so inwardly focused that they miss excellent growth opportunities and so outwardly focused that they spend shareholders' capital on hopeless ventures. (See "The Critical Questions for Diversification Success," below.)

Diversification will never be an easy game, and managers must study their cards carefully. It takes smart players to know when it's best to raise their bets and when it's best to fold.

The Critical Questions for Diversification Success

Most managers tackle the decision to diversify by using financial analysis. That's necessary but not sufficient. The six questions explored in this article are designed to help managers identify the strategic risks—and opportunities—that diversification presents.

What can our company do better than any of its competitors in its current market?

Managers often diversify on the basis of vague definitions of their business rather than on a systematic analysis of what sets their company apart from its competitors. By determining what they can do better than their existing competitors, companies will have a better chance of succeeding in new markets.

What strategic assets do we need in order to succeed in the new market?

Excelling in one market does not guarantee success in a new and related one. Managers considering diversification must ask whether their company has every strategic asset necessary to establish a competitive advantage in the territory it hopes to conquer.

Can we catch up to or leapfrog competitors at their own game?

All is not necessarily lost if managers find that they lack a critical strategic asset. There is always the potential to buy what is missing, develop it in-house, or render it unnecessary by changing the competitive rules of the game.

Will diversification break up strategic assets that need to be kept together?

Many companies introduce their time-tested strategic assets in a new market and still fail. That is because they have separated strategic assets that rely on one another for their effectiveness and hence are not able to function alone.

Will we be simply a player in the new market or will we emerge a winner?

Diversifying companies are often quickly outmaneuvered by their new competitors. Why? In many cases, they have failed to consider whether their strategic assets can be easily imitated, purchased on the open market, or replaced.

What can our company learn by diversifying, and are we sufficiently organized to learn it?

Savvy companies know how to make diversification a learning experience. They see how new businesses can help improve existing ones, act as stepping-stones to industries previously out of reach, or improve organizational efficiency.

Notes

1. See Michael E. Porter, "From Competitive Advantage to Corporate Strategy," HBR May–June 1987; David J. Collis and Cynthia A. Montgomery, "Competing on Resources: Strategy in the 1990s," HBR July–August 1995; and Andrew Campbell, Michael Goold, and Marcus Alexander, "Corporate Strategy: The Quest for Parenting Advantage," HBR March–April 1995.

2. See Theodore Levitt, "Marketing Myopia," HBR July–August 1960; C. K. Prahalad and Gary Hamel, "The Core Competence of the Corporation," HBR May–June 1990.

3. The original experiment was conducted by David Aaker and Kevin Lane Keller, and their results are presented in "Consumer Evaluations of Brand Extensions," *Journal of*

Marketing, January 1990, p. 27. The results presented here are based on a series of experiments that I carried out with 120 executives attending the Accelerated Development Programme at London Business School between 1993 and 1996.

Originally published in November–December 1997
Reprint 97608

The Living Company

ARIE DE GEUS

Executive Summary

WHAT CAN EXPLAIN THE LONGEVITY GAP between a company that survives for centuries—the Swedish company Stora, for example, which is more than 700 years old—and the average corporation, which does not last 20 years?

A team at Royal Dutch/Shell Group explored that question. Arie de Geus, a retired Shell executive, writes about the team's findings and describes what he calls *living companies*—organizations that have beaten the high mortality rate of the average corporation.

Many companies die young, de Geus argues, because their policies and practices are based too heavily on the thinking and language of economics. Their managers focus on producing goods and services and forget that the organization is a community of human beings that is in business—any business—to stay alive.

99

In contrast, managers of living companies consider themselves to be stewards of a long-standing enterprise. Their priorities reflect their commitment to the organization's long-term survival in an unpredictable world. Like careful gardeners, they encourage growth and renewal without endangering the plant they are tending. They value profits the same way most people value oxygen: as necessary for life but not the purpose of it. They scuttle assets when necessary to make a dramatic change in the business portfolio. And they constantly search for new ideas.

These managers also focus on developing people. They create opportunities for employees to learn from one another. Such organizations are suited for survival in a world in which success depends on the ability to learn, to adapt, and to evolve.

In the world of institutions, commercial corporations are newcomers. They have been around for only 500 years—a mere blip in the course of human civilization. In that time, as producers of material wealth, they have enjoyed immense success. They have sustained the world's exploding population with the goods and services that make civilized life possible.

If you look at them in light of what they could be, however, most commercial corporations are underachievers. They exist at an early stage of evolution; they develop and exploit only a small fraction of their potential. Consider their high mortality rate. By 1983, one-third of the 1970 *Fortune* 500 companies had been acquired or broken into pieces, or had merged with other companies.

How do we know that many of the deaths are premature? Because we have evidence of much greater corporate longevity. Japan's Sumitomo has its origins in a copper-casting shop founded by Riemon Soga in 1590. And the Swedish company Stora, currently a major paper, pulp, and chemical manufacturer, began as a copper mine in central Sweden more than 700 years ago. Examples such as these suggest that the natural life span of a corporation could be two or three centuries—or more.

The implications of the statistics are depressing. The gap between the endurance of a Sumitomo or a Stora and the fleeting life of the average corporation represents wasted potential. Individuals, communities, and economies are all affected—even devastated—by untimely corporate deaths. The high corporate mortality rate seems unnatural. No living species suffers from such a discrepancy between its maximum life expectancy and the average span it realizes. And few other types of institution—churches, armies, or universities—have the abysmal record of the corporation.

Why do so many companies die young? Mounting evidence suggests that corporations fail because their policies and practices are based too heavily on the thinking and the language of economics. Put another way, companies die because their managers focus exclusively on producing goods and services and forget that the organization is a community of human beings that is in business—any business—to stay alive. Managers concern themselves with land, labor, and capital, and overlook the fact that labor means real people.

What is so special about long-lived companies? "All happy families resemble one another," Tolstoy writes in *Anna Karenina*. "But each unhappy family is unhappy in its own way." What I have come to call *living companies* have a personality that allows them to evolve harmoniously. They know who they are, understand how they fit into the world, value new ideas and new people, and husband their money in a way that allows them to govern their future. Those personality traits manifest themselves in behaviors designed to renew the company over many generations. Throughout, living companies produce goods and services to earn their keep in the same way that most of us have jobs in order to live our lives.

Before i discuss the characteristics of the living company in more detail, some background is in order. In 1983, a group at Shell set out to learn something about long-term corporate survival by studying companies older than Shell. Shell was about 100 years old at the time, so we looked for companies that already existed by the fourth quarter of the nineteenth century, that were important in their industries, and that still had strong corporate identities.

Our team found 30 companies scattered throughout North America, Europe, and Japan that met those criteria. The companies ranged in age from 100 to 700 years. And 27 of them had reasonably well documented histories, including DuPont, W.R. Grace, Kodak, Mitsui, Sumitomo, and Siemens. As we all know, corporate history mostly consists of self-congratulatory books and articles written by people in the company itself about the virtues of the chief executive. The data are not always reliable. Nevertheless, we believe that those histories gave us some insights and that we learned something valuable from our study.

The first thing we learned is that the average life span of a corporation is much shorter than its potential life span. We already had an inkling of that from studying the *Fortune* 500 lists, and we obtained confirming data from registries in North America, Europe, and Japan. In most of those places, the law requires the births and deaths of companies to be registered. Through studying those registries, we acquired corporate "population statistics," which include three important bits of information: the birth rate, the death rate, and the total population. With those three pieces of information, we could calculate the average life expectancy of companies, and we found that across the Northern Hemisphere, average corporate life expectancy was well below 20 years. Only the large companies we studied, which had started to expand after they survived infancy—during which the mortality rate is extremely high—continued to live on average another 20 to 30 years.

It appears that in the corporation we have a species with a maximum life expectancy in the hundreds of years but an average life expectancy of less than 50 years. If this species were Homo sapiens, we could rightly say that it was still in the Neanderthal age—that it had not yet realized its potential. Neanderthals had an average life expectancy of approximately 30 years, but, biologically speaking, the human species has a maximum life expectancy of 100 years or more. That longevity gap is very similar to the one we found between short-lived and long-lived corporations.

The corporation is still in the Neanderthal age. It has not yet realized its potential.

The second observation from the Shell study is that living companies are very good at "management for change," as we say in modern lingo. Stora, the most dramatic example in our study, survived the Middle Ages,

the Reformation, the wars of the 1600s, the Industrial
Revolution, and the two world wars of the twentieth
century. For most of its life, it depended on runners,
horsemen, and ships instead of on telephones, airplanes,
and electronic networks to carry messages. Stora's business shifted from copper to forest exploitation, iron
smelting, hydropower, and eventually paper, wood pulp,
and chemicals. Its production technologies changed over
time from steam to internal combustion to electricity to
the microchip. And Stora continues to adapt to an ever
changing world.

WHAT DO THE EXTRAORDINARILY SUCCESSFUL
COMPANIES HAVE IN COMMON? To find out, we
looked for correlations. We know that correlations are
not always reliable; nevertheless, in the 27 survivors, our
group saw four shared personality traits that could
explain their longevity.

Conservatism in financing. The companies did not
risk their capital gratuitously. They understood the
meaning of money in an old-fashioned way; they knew
the usefulness of spare cash in the kitty. Money in hand
allowed them to snap up options when their competitors could not. They did not have to convince third-
party financiers of the attractiveness of opportunities
they wanted to pursue. Money in the kitty allowed them
to govern their growth and evolution.

Sensitivity to the world around them. Whether they
had built their fortunes on knowledge (such as DuPont's
technological innovations) or on natural resources (such

as the Hudson's Bay Company's access to the furs of Canadian forests), the living companies in our study were able to adapt themselves to changes in the world around them. As wars, depressions, technologies, and politics surged and ebbed, they always seemed to excel at keeping their feelers out, staying attuned to whatever was going on. For information, they sometimes relied on packets carried over vast distances by portage and ship, yet they managed to react in a timely fashion to whatever news they received. They were good at learning and adapting.

Awareness of their identity. No matter how broadly diversified the companies were, their employees all felt like parts of a whole. Lord Cole, chairman of Unilever in the 1960s, for example, saw the company as a fleet of ships. Each ship was independent, but the whole fleet was greater than the sum of its parts. The feeling of belonging to an organization and identifying with its achievements is often dismissed as soft. But case histories repeatedly show that a sense of community is essential for long-term survival. Managers in the living companies we studied were chosen mostly from within, and all considered themselves to be stewards of a longstanding enterprise. Their top priority was keeping the institution at least as healthy as it had been when they took over.

Tolerance of new ideas. The long-lived companies in our study tolerated activities in the margin: experiments and eccentricities that stretched their understanding. They recognized that new businesses may be entirely unrelated to existing businesses and that the act of starting a business need not be centrally controlled.

W.R. Grace, from its very beginning, encouraged autonomous experimentation. The company was founded in 1854 by an Irish immigrant in Peru and traded in guano, a natural fertilizer, before it moved into sugar and tin. Eventually, the company established Pan American Airways. Today it is primarily a chemical company, although it is also the leading provider of kidney dialysis services in the United States.

By definition, a company that survives for more than a century exists in a world it cannot hope to control. Multinational companies are similar to the long-surviving companies of our study in that way. The world of a multinational is very large and stretches across many cultures. That world is inherently less stable and more difficult to influence than a confined national habitat. Multinationals, like enduring companies, must be willing to change in order to succeed.

These four traits form the essential character of companies that have functioned successfully for hundreds of years. Given this basic personality, what priorities do the managers of living companies set for themselves and their employees?

THE MANAGER OF A LIVING COMPANY UNDER-STANDS that keeping the company alive means handing it over to a successor in at least the same health that it was in when he or she took charge. To do that, a manager must let people grow within a community that is held together by clearly stated values. The manager, therefore, must place commitment to people before assets, respect for innovation before devotion to policy, the messiness of learning before orderly procedures, and the perpetuation of the community before all other concerns.

Valuing people, not assets. This inversion of traditional managerial priorities is supported by a surprising finding in our study: each of the 27 long-lived companies changed its business portfolio completely at least once. DuPont, which is approximately 200 years old, started out as a gunpowder company. In the 1920s, it was the major shareholder of General Motors, and now DuPont is a specialty chemical company. Mitsui, which is about 300 years old, began as a drapery shop. It then became a bank, went into mining, and at the end of the nineteenth century, the company moved into manufacturing.

Those histories tell me that such companies are willing to scuttle assets in order to survive. To them, assets—and profits—are like oxygen: necessary for life but not the purpose of life. Stora was in copper in order to exist; it did not exist to be in copper. These companies know that assets are just means to earning a living. A company run according to a different model scuttles people to save its plant and equipment, which it considers the essence of its being. If such a company were in the car rental business today, for example, it would see itself as existing to rent cars. The company's fleet would be considered its primary asset, and its purpose would be to make profits for shareholders. If such companies find themselves in trouble, they get rid of people.

Loosening steering and control. If long-term corporate health and survival across generations require a willingness to change the business portfolio, managers must heed the opinions and practices of other people. The organization must give people the space to develop ideas. They must have some freedom from control, from direction, and from punishment for failures. In other words, managers must put the principle of tolerance into practice by taking risks with people and looking in new places in search of fresh ideas. Perhaps the best way to illustrate that notion is through the metaphor of rose gardening.

If you're a gardener, every spring you must decide how you will prune your roses: hard or long. Pruning hard means that you select three of the plant's strongest stems and cut them down to three or four growth buds. That technique forces the plant to channel all its resources into a relatively small number of growth buds. Why would you prune your roses in that way? Because you want the biggest roses in the neighborhood in June.

If I prune hard and the nights are frosty and the deer are hungry, I might not have any roses.

I don't prune hard. Why? Because it's a high-risk strategy. Where I live, the most terrible things can happen to my roses. I live on a hill, where night frosts in April or even early May are not uncommon. Also, many deer roam freely on the hill, and they love to eat rosebuds. If I prune hard and the nights are frosty and the deer are hungry, I might have no roses in June at all. So I prune long: I leave between five and seven stems on each plant, and on each stem I leave between five and seven growth buds. As a result, the plant is allowed to spread its resources over many growth buds. I have never had the biggest roses in the neighborhood, but I do have roses every June.

And something else happens when you prune long for a number of years: you get surprises. In two or three years, some of the spindlier stems have grown much stronger and have begun producing buds, and some of the old stems do not produce roses anymore. So what do you do? You remove the old stems and encourage the new ones. A tolerant pruning policy gradually renews the rose portfolio.

The gardening metaphor also helps resolve one of modern management's dilemmas: how to diversify without courting disaster. A policy of tolerance allows the rose and the environment to engage each other continually without endangering the rose's capacity for growth.

Organizing for learning.   There are times when a company's know-how, product range, and labor relations are in harmony with the world around it. The business situations are familiar, the company is well organized, and employees are trained and prepared. During those times, managers do not need to develop and implement new ideas. Their job is to allocate resources to promote growth and development, channeling capital and people to the parts of the organization best positioned to benefit from the current state of affairs. Those parts of the organization then become larger, better established, and more powerful.

But just when the company has organized itself, outside circumstances may change. New technologies come on the scene, markets shift, interest rates fluctuate, consumers' tastes change, and the company must enter a new phase of life. In

Once a company has adapted to a new environment, it is no longer the same company. It has evolved.

order to stay in sync with the outside world, it must be able to alter its marketing strategy, its product range, its organizational form, and where and how it does its manufacturing. And once a company has adapted to a new environment, it is no longer the organization it used to be; it has evolved. That is the essence of learning.

How does an organization—as distinct from an individual—learn? Birds can help us answer that question. Consider the work of Allan Wilson, the late professor of biochemistry and molecular biology at the University of California at Berkeley. According to Wilson's hypothesis, an entire species can improve its ability to exploit the opportunities in its environment. Three conditions are necessary. First, the members of the species must have and use the ability to move around, and they must flock or move in herds rather than sit individually in isolated territories. Second, some of the individuals must have the potential to invent new behaviors—new skills. Third, the species must have an established process for transmitting a skill from the individual to the entire community, not genetically but through direct communication. The presence of those three conditions, according to Wilson, will accelerate learning in the species as a whole, increasing its ability to adapt quickly to fundamental changes in the environment.

To test his hypothesis, Wilson revisited a well-documented account of the behavior of titmice and red robins in Great Britain. In the late nineteenth century, milkmen left open bottles of milk outside people's doors. A rich cream would rise to the tops of the bottles. Two garden birds common in Great Britain, titmice and red robins, began to eat the cream.

In the 1930s, after the birds had been enjoying the cream for about 50 years, the British put aluminum seals on the milk bottles. What happened? By the early 1950s, the entire estimated population of one million titmice in Great Britain, from Scotland to Land's End, had learned to pierce the seals. The robins never acquired that skill.

Why did titmice gain the advantage in the inter-
species competition? Remember that Wilson identified
the conditions necessary for learning to take place in a
population: numerous mobile individuals, some of
whom are innovative, and a social system for propagat-
ing innovation. The red robins lacked such a social system. Of course, robins sing, have color, and are mobile—
they can communicate. But they are fundamentally
territorial birds. Four or five robins live in my garden,
and each has its own small territory. There's a lot of
communication among them, but what they usually
have to say to one another is, Get out. Titmice also love
my garden. They live together in pairs in May and June.
By the end of June and July, you see the titmice in flocks
of 8, 10, and 12. They fly from garden to garden, and they
play and feed.

Birds that flock learn faster. So do organizations that
encourage flocking behavior. Any organization with several hundred employees is bound to have at least a couple of people curious
enough to poke their way
into new places, like titmice finding their cream.
But keeping a few innova-
tors on hand is not
enough to ensure institutional learning. The organization must encourage those people to interact with others. Skunk works are an example of that phenomenon.

*Birds that flock learn
faster. So do organizations
that encourage their
employees to flock.*

Management development programs are also an
excellent opportunity for flocking. Shell, for instance,
spends about $2,400 per employee each year on training
that helps employees advance in their fields, move into
new endeavors, and develop new skills. Even more significant, most of the training is collaborative. It is very

important for teams of disparate people to undergo intensive training together at regular intervals. Such an experience helps disseminate knowledge across an organization and brings together people from various cultural backgrounds and professional and academic disciplines. The flocking is intensive. Course attendees nearly always report afterward, "It was not so much what I learned in the official sessions but what I picked up from my colleagues during the breaks that was important."

Shaping the human community. Managers must decide how to position the human element in their companies. They can choose to produce wealth for an inner circle of managers and investors, or they can develop an organization that is a community. The choice they make plays a large role in determining whether a company will outlive its founders. Managers who want to build an organization that can survive many generations pay attention to the development of employees above all other considerations. They give a high priority to questions such as, How can we organize for continuity from one generation to the next?

In organizations in which benefits accrue to only a few people, all others are outsiders, not members. According to their underlying contract with the company, those outsiders trade their time and expertise for money. As ample evidence from the organizational behavioral sciences shows, that type of contract does not inspire people to give their all or to feel much loyalty to the enterprise or its managers. Recruits understand that they should work with their eventual exit in mind. Succession in those companies is difficult and costly. The company's continuity over generations is not ensured.

To me, a company whose purpose is to produce wealth for a few people is like a puddle of rainwater—a collection of raindrops that pool in a cavity or hollow. The drops remain at the bottom of the cavity. When it rains, more drops may be added to the puddle and its field of influence may broaden, soaking the ground around it. But the original drops remain in the middle.

Stasis can lead to vulnerability. Puddles of water cannot survive much heat. When the sun comes out and the temperature rises, the puddle starts evaporating. Even the drops in the center are in danger of going up in vapor.

The company whose purpose is survival is more like a river. Unlike a puddle, a river is a permanent feature of the landscape. Come rain, the river may swell. Come shine, it may shrink. But it takes a long and severe drought for a river to disappear. From the point of view of the drops of water, the river is quite turbulent. No drop remains at the center for long. From one moment to the next, the water in one part of the river changes. New water drops succeed old ones, and they all are carried forward.

The river lasts many times longer than the individual drops of water it comprises. The river is a self-perpetuating community with its own built-in guarantees for the continuity and motion of water within its banks. A company, by initiating rules for the continuity and motion of its people, can emulate the river's longevity and power.

The living company is a river company. In such an organization, managers regard the optimization of capital as no more than a necessary complement to the optimization of people. To build a company that is profitable and will live long, managers take care to create a community. Processes are in place to define membership, establish common values, recruit people, develop employees, assess individual potential, live up to a human contract, and establish policies for graceful exits from the company.

Above all, in the living company, members know "who is us," and they are aware that they hold values in common. They know the answer to the definitive question about corporate identity: What do we value? Whoever cannot live with the company's values cannot and should not be a member. The sense of belonging pulls together even the most diverse members of the company.

In the living company, the essence of the underlying contract is mutual trust. Individuals understand that in exchange for their effort and commitment, the company will help them develop their potential. Money is not considered a positive motivator in a river company. If money is insufficient, people will become dissatisfied, but adding money above the threshold of sufficient pay will not motivate people to give more to the company. Before they will give more, people need to know that the community is interested in them as individuals, and they themselves need to be interested in the fate of the enterprise. Both the entity and the individual need to care more about each other.

Part of that caring is making sure that people enter and exit the company with the right understanding. Recruits are judged as much on the basis of their fit with the company's values and principles as they are on their ability to fulfill the technical requirements of the job. People are hired into a living company with the understanding that they are there to develop their potential. This does not mean that they have a contract for life. If people don't pull their weight or share the community's values, they must move on. And when they reach a certain age, it is time for them to go. Leadership in living companies is the opposite of that portrayed in the old cartoon that shows 12 geriatric board members nodding slowly to the chairman, who is proposing to extend the retirement age by one year.

One benefit of strict exit rules is that management becomes stewardship. Just as you took over from somebody, you will pass the baton to someone else. Your legacy at the company will depend on how well you carried out your stewardship.

MANY SHAREHOLDERS AND SENIOR MANAGERS are not interested in building a self-perpetuating work community. They prefer the company to remain a moneymaking machine for the benefit of an inner circle. Theirs is a perfectly legitimate choice, but those who make that choice must realize that there is no free lunch.

More and more companies operate in a world they do not control. The chances that a company can influence today's world to its benefit grow smaller every day—as banks, insurance companies, telecommunications companies, and software makers are finding out. Why? Because global competition is forcing companies to move out of their regional or national niches into less familiar territory. Even companies that do not expand find the outside world invading their turf. In the global village, it is increasingly difficult to find niches or hide behind barriers. In short, corporate money machines risk becoming an endangered species capable of living only in protected national parks.

Living, learning companies stand a better chance of surviving and evolving in a world they do not control.

They make sense, especially because success now depends on mobilizing as much of the intelligence at a company's disposal as possible. The high levels of tolerance inside the living organization create the space for more innovation and learning. Creating that space is vital for brain-rich, asset-poor companies like law and accounting firms, credit card companies, and financial services companies, whose success depends on the quality of their internal communities. But even the old type of asset-rich company, such as oil and car companies, need much more knowledge embedded in their products and services now than they did 20 years ago.

The living company stands a better chance of living longer—of reducing the gap between the average and maximum life expectancy of the corporate species. Why does that matter? Because the death of a company is not without costs. Employees, suppliers, contractors, communities, and shareholders all feel the loss.

Originally published in March–April 1997
Reprint 97203

Making the Deal Real

How GE Capital Integrates Acquisitions

RONALD N. ASHKENAS,
LAWRENCE J. DEMONACO,
AND SUZANNE C. FRANCIS

Executive Summary

MOST COMPANIES VIEW ACQUISITIONS AND MERG-
ERS as onetime events managed with heroic effort—
anxiety-producing experiences that often result in lost
jobs, restructured responsibilities, derailed careers, and
diminished power. Little wonder, then, that most managers think about how to get them over with—not how to
do them better. But even as the number of mergers and
acquisitions rises in the United States, studies show the
performance of the resulting companies falls below
industry averages more often than not.

To improve these statistics, executives need to view
acquisition integration as a manageable process, not a
unique event. One company that has done exactly that
is GE Capital Services, which has assimilated more than
100 acquisitions in the past five years alone and, in the

process, has developed a formal model for melding new acquisitions into the corporate fold.

Drawing on their experiences working with the company to develop the model, consultants Ron Ashkenas and Suzanne Francis, together with GE Capital's Lawrence DeMonaco, offer four lessons from the company's successful run. First, begin the integration process before the deal is signed. Second, dedicate a full-time individual to managing the integration process. Third, implement any necessary restructuring sooner rather than later. And fourth, integrate not only the business operations but also the corporate cultures. These guidelines won't erase all of the discomfort that accompanies many mergers, but they can make the process more transparent and predictable for those involved.

LIKE THE PROCESS BY WHICH A CHILD LEARNS TO WALK, most business innovations emerge from dozens of trial-and-error experiments; from seemingly random actions that eventually form a pattern; from hundreds of small, almost imperceptible adjustments that eventually result in a solid step forward. This has been true for developments ranging from lean manufacturing to concurrent product development to business process reengineering—all now well-accepted innovations that emerged from dozens of experiments until they crystallized to form a methodology others could follow.

An exception to this rule thus far has been innovation relating to acquisition integration—the process by which one company melds with another after the deal is done. Most acquisitions and mergers are onetime events that companies manage with heroic effort; few companies go through the process often enough to develop a pattern. Thus it tends to be seen not as a process—as something replicable—but only as something to get finished, so everyone can get back to business.

The tendency to see integration as a unique event in an organization's life is magnified by the fact that acquisitions and mergers often are painful and anxiety-producing experiences. *No wonder most managers think about how to get acquisitions over with—not how to do them better.* They involve job loss, restructured responsibilities, derailed careers, diminished power, and much else that is stressful. No wonder most managers think about how to get them over with—not how to do them better the next time.

Improving the acquisition integration process, however, may be one of the most urgent and compelling challenges facing businesses today. Industry consolidations, the globalization of competition, technological developments, and other trends have touched off an unprecedented wave of mergers and acquisitions that shows no signs of abating. According to figures from the Securities Data Company published in the *New York Times*, the dollar value of U.S. mergers and acquisitions announced in 1996 alone grew more than 27% to $658.8 billion from $518 billion in 1995.

Despite this enormous growth in merger activity, acquisitions that appear to be both financially and strategically sound on paper often turn out to be disappointing for many companies: the acquiring company takes too many years to realize the expected synergies or is unable to get people to work together productively or puts the companies together in such a heavy-handed way that the unique capabilities of the acquired company (its best people and most valued customers, for example) melt away. Perhaps that's why a study reported last January in the *Economist* of 300 major mergers conducted over a ten-year period by Mercer Management Consulting found that in 57% of these merged companies return to shareholders lagged behind the average for their industries.

Given this confluence of events—a growing number of mergers and acquisitions combined with high failure rates—it is increasingly important that executives learn how to manage the integration of acquisitions as a replicable process and not as a onetime-only event. One company to learn from is GE Capital Services—an organization that has made more than 100 acquisitions in the past five years, resulting in a 30% increase in its workforce, the rapid globalization of its businesses, and a doubling of its net income. GE Capital has been working to make acquisition integration a core capability and a competitive advantage that will enable it to continue its growth in the future.

For the past three years, we have been part of a team that has helped GE Capital learn from its extensive acquisition-integration experience to create a more replicable process. We have interviewed dozens of managers and staff members from both acquiring and acquired businesses, including many who after being acquired by GE Capital became acquirers themselves. Using these interviews and related documents and materials, we have helped GE Capital create a model for acquisition integration. This model has been fine-tuned through workshops with GE Capital's many acquisition-integration experts, and it has been applied successfully to several recent integration efforts. (See the exhibit "The Wheel of Fortune.")

Growth Through Acquisition

To appreciate the lessons GE Capital has learned about acquisition integration, it is important to understand that GE Capital itself is the product of dozens of acquisitions that have been blended to form one of the world's largest financial-services organizations.

GE Capital was founded in 1933 as a subsidiary of the General Electric Company to provide consumers with credit to purchase GE appliances. Since then, the company has grown to become a major financial-services conglomerate with 27 separate businesses, more than 50,000 employees worldwide (nearly half of them outside the United States), and a net income in 1996 of $2.8 billion. The businesses that generate these returns range from private-label credit-card services to commercial real-estate financing to railcar and aircraft leasing. More than half of these businesses became part of GE Capital through acquisitions.

For the past decade, since Gary Wendt became chairman of GE Capital, the company's plans for growth have included acquiring companies. Thus every business is constantly seeking acquisitions. To engineer these deals, each executive vice president (who heads a group of businesses) has a Business Development, or BD, officer. Larger businesses within each group have their own BD officer, and Wendt also has BD people on his staff. Those professionals, many from consulting firms, focus on finding, analyzing, and negotiating acquisitions that will contribute to GE Capital's growth.

The acquisitions come in different shapes and sizes. Sometimes, the acquisition is a portfolio or asset purchase that adds volume to a particular business without adding people. Sometimes, it is a consolidating acquisition in which a company is purchased and then

The Wheel of Fortune

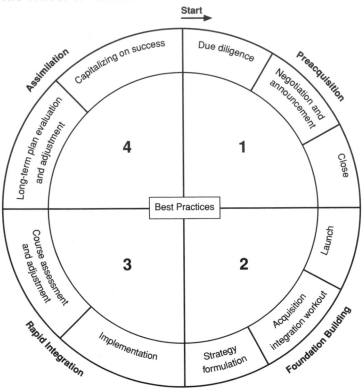

Over the years, GE Capital Services' acquisition-integration process has been discussed, debated, tested, changed, and refined. It is now established well enough to be codified in what we call the Pathfinder Model.

The model divides the process into four "action stages," starting with the work that goes on before the acquisition is completed — that is, before the deal closes — and continuing all the way through assimilation. There are two or three subprocesses in each action stage, such as due diligence during the preacquisition stage and strategy formulation during the foundation-building stage. Finally, each action stage includes several best practices — specific and practical steps managers can take to support the process.

The model's neat and systematic appearance belies the fact that acquisition integration is as much art as science. The Pathfinder Model recommends a particular sequence of leveraged actions, but there are aspects of every acquisition-integration process that are new or unique. As in any major organizational transformation, managers will have to improvise. The model, however, can prevent improvisation from becoming the whole show.

consolidated into an existing GE Capital business. That happened when GE Capital Vendor Financial Services bought Chase Manhattan Bank's leasing business. Sometimes, the acquisition moves into fresh territory, spawning an entirely new GE Capital business. GE Capital made such a "platform," or strategic, acquisition when it bought the Travelers Corporation's Mortgage Services business. And finally, sometimes, the acquisition is a

---

The Wheel of Fortune (continued)

1. **Preacquisition**
   - Begin cultural assessment
   - Identify business/cultural barriers to integration success
   - Select integration manager
   - Assess strengths/weaknesses of business and function leaders
   - Develop communication strategy

2. **Foundation Building**
   - Formally introduce integration manager
   - Orient new executives to GE Capital business rhythms and nonnegotiables
   - Jointly formulate integration plan, including 100-day and communication plans
   - Visibly involve senior management
   - Provide sufficient resources and assign accountability

3. **Rapid Integration**
   - Use process mapping, CAP, and Workout to accelerate integration
   - Use audit staff for process audits
   - Use feedback and learning to continually adapt integration plan
   - Initiate short-term management exchange

4. **Assimilation**
   - Continue developing common tools, practices, processes, and language
   - Continue longer-term management exchanges
   - Utilize corporate education center and Crotonville
   - Use audit staff for integration audit

hybrid, parts of which fit into one or more existing businesses while other parts stand alone or become joint ventures.

From these acquisitions, and its efforts to make them work on a financial and organizational basis, GE Capital has learned the following four lessons:

LESSON 1

Acquisition integration is not a discrete phase of a deal and does not begin when the documents are signed. Rather, it is a process that begins with due diligence and runs through the ongoing management of the new enterprise.

Any manager who has been involved with an acquisition will agree that the process proceeds through a number of fairly predictable stages: selecting possible acquisitions, narrowing the field, agreeing on a first-choice candidate, assessing compliance with regulations, convening preliminary discussions, formulating a letter of intent, conducting due diligence, completing financial negotiations, making the announcement, signing the agreement, and closing the deal. And given these stages, it is natural to assume that integration would begin after the deal is closed.

For many years, GE Capital, like most organizations, proceeded under that assumption. Business development specialists, working with business leaders and finance experts, saw most of the deals through to closing. After the documents were signed and the mementos exchanged, managers were expected to take over and begin the integration process.

The realization that integration is not a stage following the deal came about through experience.

Unfortunately, in most cases, that approach to integration was less than effective. Integration was slow and costly. There were constant surprises about peoples' reactions to being acquired, and financial returns were often hindered by delays in putting the companies together. In some cases, when acquisitions did succeed, it was mainly because the acquired company was left alone and not integrated into GE Capital.

Necessity mothers invention. Like most things an organization learns, the realization that integration is not a stage following the deal, and could be done faster and more effectively if it were begun sooner, came about through experience. In the mid-1980s, GE Capital acquired Dart & Kraft Leasing and Kerr Leasing, intending to integrate Kerr into D&K. In the midst of that integration process, GE Capital acquired Gelco Corporation, a much larger leasing company that also included other financial-services businesses. At that point, the acquisition strategy called for integrating both D&K and Kerr into Gelco's auto-fleet-leasing business, spinning off some other pieces of Gelco into freestanding businesses, and selling some nonstrategic pieces of the company.

In short, this was no simple acquisition integration, and many of GE Capital's senior executives were concerned that the standard approaches to integration would be inadequate.

As a response, a human resources executive suggested that the company's communication expert use the regulatory review period before the Gelco acquisition closed to create a comprehensive communication plan for the forthcoming integration. But instead of just a communication plan, what emerged was the framework for an entire integration strategy. That strategy included a 48-hour communication blitz directed at employees immediately after the deal closed; the formulation of a role in the new organization for the former Gelco, D&K, and Kerr executives; a strategy for presenting the acquisition to the media; a way to handle some necessary consolidations of headquarters staff; and an outplacement plan.

Most important, the framework signaled a new way of thinking about integration—a recognition that there were predictable issues that could be anticipated long before the deal actually closed. The Gelco acquisition turned out to be a watershed for GE Capital, a demonstration that extremely complex transactions could be assimilated more successfully by planning for integration well before the closing.

Integrating: earlier is better. Eventually, the planning process began to extend back even further—into the due diligence phase—as GE Capital executives realized that thinking about integration that early could speed the eventual melding. In the early 1990s, that thinking was formalized during due diligence for a Chicago-based equipment-leasing company. The head of the due diligence effort, having seen how effective the Gelco plan had been, convened a series of end-of-day meetings for the functional captains of the various due-diligence teams (including finance, operations, systems, human resources, and sales) to discuss what they had learned each day and to develop preliminary plans for managing the acquisition after the deal closed.

Applying those lessons to subsequent acquisitions, GE Capital found that being sensitive to integration issues during the due diligence phase began to foster better decisions about whether to proceed with an acquisition at all. During the final stages of due diligence for the acquisition of a British leasing-equipment company, for example, two senior business leaders from GE Capital had a working lunch with the CEO and CFO of the company, expressly to discuss some of GE Capital's expectations for how the merged company would be run.

Recognizing that planning for integration can begin with the very first discussions gave GE Capital a head start.

During lunch, significant differences in basic management styles and values became clear. The conversation led GE Capital to take a harder look at the management culture of the target company and to realize that integration could be difficult and contentious. On that basis, despite very favorable financials, GE Capital walked away from the transaction.

Today recognizing that planning for integration can begin with the very first discussions gives GE Capital a head start in bringing new companies into the fold. For example, during investigations relating to the credit card business of a major European retailer, the due diligence team learned that employees of the soon-to-be-acquired company were concerned that they might lose their traditional shopping-discount benefit at the retailer's stores. GE Capital persuaded the retailer to continue the discount for one year after the acquisition and also agreed to make up the difference of the lost benefit in subsequent years by adding approximately $200 to each employee's paycheck. As a result, GE Capital turned a potential cause of friction into a positive experience that led to boosted morale (as measured through attitude surveys), greater receptivity to other changes, and higher productivity.

LESSON 2

Integration management is a full-time job and needs to be recognized as a distinct business function, just like operations, marketing, or finance.

Since acquisition integration is an ongoing process and not a discrete stage of a deal, someone needs to manage it. That may seem obvious, but in reality the issue is complex—one that GE Capital has grappled with for more than a decade.

Let's look at the key players in an acquisition: The acquiring business usually will have a due diligence team that includes people from such areas as finance, tax, business development, human resources, and technology. It will have a "leader" (GE's term for a general manager) who is the ultimate "buyer" of the company. Similarly, the acquired business will have a business leader and a full complement of managers and staff.

Who among that cast of characters focuses on integration? Who is the one person responsible for making sure that the new company becomes a fully functioning, high-performing part of the acquirer?

For many years at GE Capital, the answer to that question was unclear. The due diligence team, which developed the deepest knowledge of the new company and had the best insight into what would be needed to integrate it after the deal closed, usually disbanded after the deal was struck, its members returning to their regular jobs or moving on to the next transaction. The functional and business leaders of the acquiring GE company typically focused only on the integration of their particular units. The newly acquired business leaders, who had the most incentive to integrate and learn how to be successful with their new owners, did not have sufficient knowledge of GE Capital, its resources, or its integration requirements. What's more, they tended to be preoccupied with running the company and also with a host of personal issues—protecting, reassuring, or outplacing their people; figuring out whether they wanted to stay in the new company; and (perhaps unconsciously) proving that their company was even better than the buyers thought.

Given those realities, the business leader of the acquiring GE business was usually assumed to be accountable for integration. But for a number of reasons, that was an unrealistic assignment. In most cases, the business leader had other units to run and was not dedicated fully to the new acquisition. And even when the business leader was able to devote time to the acquisition, his or her focus usually was not on integrating the cultures, processes, and people but, appropriately, on such critical business issues as profit growth, staffing key jobs, and customer retention.

Furthermore, the business leader's very position of authority often limited his or her ability to facilitate integration. People in a newly acquired company need someone they can talk to freely, to ask "stupid" questions, find out how things work at GE Capital, and discover what resources are available and how to use them. They need a guide to the new culture and a bridge between their company and GE Capital. The last person who fits that role is the new boss they want to impress.

A role is born. At GE Capital, the role of designated integration manager evolved, as most innovations do, through a combination of chance and necessity. Consider, again, the case of Gelco. At the time, it was GE Capital's largest acquisition. Larry Toole, a senior human-resources executive who had been involved in the due diligence effort, was asked to stay on and support the newly acquired Gelco team. Toole (now GE Capital's head of human resources) acted as a facilitator to the new leadership team. He brought groups of people from GE Capital and Gelco together in work sessions to develop common plans; he oriented the new team to GE Capital's requirements; he made sure that the soft sides of the integration (such as communication and benefits) were taken into account; and he counseled Gelco's senior managers about how to succeed in GE Capital.

By the end of the 1980s, it was clear that the Gelco integration had gone well. But the critical role that Toole had played as an integration manager was not fully recognized until several other acquisitions that had no integration managers failed to proceed as smoothly. For example, no integration manager was assigned when GE Capital's retail credit-card business bought the credit card operations of the Burton Group (a U.K. retailer) in 1991. Two years later, when the unit was not meeting expectations, a reintegration effort, which did include a full-time integration manager, turned the situation around.

By 1994, it was apparent that the integration manager was a key role. Then the questions became, Who would make a good integration manager? and How should the job actually work?

An accidental role becomes an intentional strategy. Today two types of people are generally selected to be integration managers in GE Capital—the *high-potential* individual and the *experienced hand.* The high-potential manager is usually a less seasoned person with strong functional credentials who is viewed as a future business leader. That type of person is widely employed in small, straightforward, or highly structured integration efforts. For more complex acquisitions or those that incorporate multiple businesses, an experienced hand—someone who knows GE Capital well and has proven management skills—usually takes on the integration job.

In all cases, the integration managers that have been most effective have been those that have served on the due diligence team. The integration manager then becomes a full-fledged member of the leadership team for the acquired business, reporting directly to its business leader. Selection of the integration manager is based as much on personal characteristics as on technical skills. In the past several years, the backgrounds of successful integration managers have been drawn from fields as diverse as human resources, auditing, finance, technology, marketing, and law. Some need to be skilled in a second language. But all have strong interpersonal skills and are sensitive to cultural differences. All have the ability to facilitate groups and a deep knowledge of how GE Capital works. And all have the energy to do what it takes to make an integration successful. (See "What It Takes to Be an Integration Manager," on page 146.)

Given the job's broad range of responsibilities, it would seem natural to hold the integration manager accountable for the performance of the business. But GE Capital's experience suggests that doing so reduces the accountability of both the business leader and the rest of the leadership team. And in reality, the integration manager does not control the critical business resources. Instead of having P&L responsibility then, most of GE Capital's integration managers are held accountable for the creation and delivery of a disciplined integration plan and for reaching the plan's milestones. In reaching those milestones, the integration manager acts more as a consultant than anything else. The job is to build connective tissue between GE Capital and the new organization, tissue that will allow information and resources to pass freely back and forth, tissue that will become self-generating over time.

An example from a European acquisition illustrates how the integration manager builds connective tissue. After completing the acquisition, the business leader asked the integration manager to quickly introduce the new company to GE's integrity policy. At GE, integrity is not just embodied in a standard corporate-policy statement. It is a detailed requirement meant to ensure that every employee understands what constitutes proper and improper ways of conducting business.

Given the importance of the integrity policy, the business leader expected that the material would be immediately reprinted, distributed, and used in dozens of meetings mandatory for all employees. But the integration manager took another tack. He asked a few senior managers from the new company how people would react to GE's policy. The response was a surprise: "If we send that out, it will be like saying to our people that before GE came along we didn't have any integrity!"

To avoid such a reaction, the integration manager quickly commissioned a small group of managers and staff members to develop a constructive way to convey the integrity policy. The group decided that its own managers (rather than GE's people) should introduce the policy at a series of all-employee meetings. They introduced those meetings by saying, "One of the benefits of belonging to GE is that they have made explicit the principles of integrity that we have always followed in our company but that we never had the resources to write down. And here they are . . ."

That may seem like a small matter, but the accumulation of such small matters can destroy the connective tissue between companies. The job of the integration manager is to keep that tissue growing.

LESSON 3

Decisions about management structure, key roles, reporting relationships, layoffs, restructuring, and other career-affecting aspects of the integration should be made, announced, and implemented as soon as possible after the deal is signed—within days, if possible. Creeping changes, uncertainty, and anxiety that last for months are debilitating and immediately start to drain value from an acquisition.

With all the tension of a medieval passion play, at the moment that an acquisition closes, an intense drama begins to unfold between the new owners and their new employees. On one side of the stage are the acquirer's managers, who almost always believe they can run the acquired company better—whether through the introduction of new capital, new technology, new resources, new energy, or new ideas. And since acquisitions come at a price, one aspect of their agenda almost always is to reduce costs.

Playing opposite the new managers are all the employees of the acquired company—from senior management to shipping-dock staff. Their script tells them that when companies are purchased, the acquiring company often puts its own people in charge, changes policies and procedures, restructures, consolidates, and generally takes over. So they walk onto the stage of the new company feeling anxious, insecure, uncertain, and even angry. Who are these new owners? What are their intentions? Can we trust what they say? Do we still have jobs, and are they the same as before? Why did our previous owners sell? Did we do a bad job, or did they betray us?

In short, the acquiring managers close the deal with a certain amount of euphoria, ready to get on with the exciting challenge of running the new business better. But the staff members needed to keep things running and make improvements are preoccupied with issues of security and identity. They have no interest in a close-the-deal party; they just want to know if they still have jobs.

If left unrecognized, this psychodrama can be debilitating and can send the integration process down the wrong path. On one hand, when issues of security are not addressed immediately, levels of productivity, customer service, and innovation quickly deteriorate as employees focus on their own needs rather than on those of the company. On the other hand, if acquiring managers restructure quickly but without sensitivity, they risk beginning their tenure without the trust and respect of the remaining staff. The challenge is to avoid both traps, to make structural changes as quickly as possible but in a way that maintains everyone's dignity. If that challenge is not met, successful integration may not be possible.

First things first: Do I have a job? Most acquisitions involve restructuring, either to improve the efficiency of the acquired unit or to ensure that its organization fits with that of the new owner. But moving quickly to restructure is not easy, even when obvious changes need to be made. Often the new owners fear that early layoffs will send the signal that they are the "bad guys." So they delay the inevitable until the "right" time. Or the new owners may worry about the publicity and the potential impact on their company's image—so they, too, wait to make layoffs, imagining that they can be made quietly later, when no one is watching. And in some situations, the new owners worry that they do not have enough experience with the company and its staff, that they will make mistakes. So they want to wait until they get to know everyone and understand the company better.

For many years, GE Capital struggled both with the challenge of finding the right time to restructure acquisitions and with the decision of when, or if, to bring in new managers. Sometimes, structural moves were delayed for many months after the company had been bought. The realization that this was a mistake came in 1991, one year after the acquisition of a finance company in Europe. It was obvious when the company was purchased that restructuring was needed. Twelve layers of management (which worked out to one manager for every two employees) had created a high-cost, high-control organization whose ability to innovate and change was highly limited. Yet despite the obvious need for "de-layering" and cost reduction, GE Capital kept all the members of the management team in place and allowed them to keep the organization intact. That was done for a number of seemingly rational reasons: fear of destroying morale, lack of confidence about which managers to let go, and a feeling that here was a European culture that GE Capital perhaps did not fully understand.

A year passed. Costs remained high, and performance remained low. Finally, GE Capital's business leader stepped in and forced a thorough consolidation. The surprise was the staff's reaction. Instead of being upset, most employees (as reported in surveys) wondered why GE Capital had taken so long. They had seen the need for cost reduction from the beginning and had spent much of the year waiting for the plans to be announced.

We have interviewed ten CEOs of companies that GE Capital has acquired from different countries about the pace of consolidation. All have said the same thing: "Although at the time we thought that things were moving too quickly, in retrospect, you did not go fast enough." In short, they said that there is no such thing as an acquisition that does not include some degree of change—in either structure, philosophy, systems, or strategy. Their message was this: if change is inevitable, let's get on with it rather than allow anxiety and speculation to diffuse energy and focus.

Restructure with respect. A crucial springboard to successful integration is the manner in which restructuring is carried out. First and foremost, the acquiring company needs to be straightforward about what is happening and what is planned. Even when the news is bad, the one thing the staff of newly acquired companies appreciates most is the truth. That includes being able to say "we don't know" about certain areas or "we have not yet decided" about others. It also includes sharing information about when and by

Never tell the acquired staff that it will be "business as usual" when it never will be again.

what process a decision may be reached. The truth also means acknowledging some of the stress and other emotions. As one CEO of an acquired company wisely noted, "Never tell the acquired staff that it will be 'business as usual' when it will never be the same for them again. And don't tell them that this was a 'merger of equals' when you have clearly taken them over. And don't tell them that they have 'a wonderful future' to look forward to when they are still confused and grieving over the past."

Second, it is critical to treat those individuals who will be negatively affected with dignity, respect, and support. Not only is this the right thing to do, it is also a powerful way to show those who remain what kind of company they now are working for—and to help them develop positive feelings.

But the most powerful way to move ahead is to get the employees of the acquired company focused on the real work of growing the newly formed business. How to shift the focus toward the future, and get people to start working on it, is the last lesson from GE Capital's experience.

LESSON 4

A successful integration melds not only the various technical aspects of the businesses but also the different cultures. The best way to do so is to get people working together quickly to solve business problems and accomplish results that could not have been achieved before.

In many ways, an acquisition is like an arranged marriage: the "parents" negotiate the deal, sign the contract, and then expect the "newlyweds" to live together in harmony. An arranged marriage, however, has a much better chance of success than an acquisition does since only one couple is involved, and the parties usually come from similar cultures and share common values. In acquisitions, many people—sometimes thousands—

need to learn how to live together, and the values and mind-sets of the acquiring and acquired organizations almost always differ. That disparity is even more marked when the two companies are based in different national cultures.

One vital issue when integrating any acquisition, then, is how to speed the process of getting dozens, hundreds, or thousands of people to work together in harmony. How do you get people from different cultures, who may even have been competitors, to build a new company that will grow and prosper?

From its experience, GE Capital has distilled four steps business leaders can take to bridge the cultural gaps that exist when integrating any acquisition. We have found that failing to take steps like these to address the "soft" side of integration turns the "hard" aspects of integration—such as reconciling different financial-accounting practices—into mechanical exercises that are executed without understanding or finesse, and often without success.

Meet, greet, and plan (urgently). Once the deal is closed and the transfer of ownership becomes official, the GE Capital business leader, with the help of the acquisition manager, organizes orientation and planning sessions for the members of the management team of the new acquisition and their counterparts in GE Capital. The intent is to use these sessions to create a 100–day plan for acquisition integration. These sessions help welcome the new senior managers into GE Capital and give them a chance to socialize with their new colleagues. They also provide an opportunity for both sides to exchange information and share their feelings and reactions about the recently completed deal.

As part of the information exchange, the newly acquired managers are asked to talk about their organization, products, people, and plans. In particular, they are asked to talk about the positive aspects of their company—what they feel good about and what should be built upon. They are then asked to share their thoughts about opportunities for improvement—what could be changed, areas of potential growth, and synergies with GE Capital.

Following that exchange, the GE Capital business leader, the integration manager, and other executives describe what it means to be a part of GE Capital—the values, the responsibilities, the challenges, and the rewards. That includes a presentation and discussion of the standards required of a GE Capital business unit, including a list of approximately 25 policies and practices that need to be incorporated into the way the acquired company does business. Those range from quarterly operating reviews to risk policies to quality and integrity procedures.

Drawing on the standards set by GE Capital and the opportunities for improvement presented by the acquired management team, the group then begins to draft the 100-day plan for acquisition integration. As its name implies, the plan outlines what will be done in the first 100 days to bring the new company into GE Capital. The plan addresses such issues as the need for integrating functions, taking any steps necessary for financial and procedural compliance, making any shifts in compensation and benefits, and managing customer contacts. The 100-day timetable creates a sense of urgency, challenge, and excitement; it imbues the integration with a feeling of zest and energy. At the same time, it forces the management team to move into action and avoid becoming paralyzed by mixed feelings and personal politics.

Communicate, communicate—and then communicate some more. Creating a communication plan during the due diligence and negotiation phases of a transaction so that employees and external parties are informed as soon as a deal is closed is only the first step in an effective communication program. Keeping the communication process going—and making it reach broadly and deeply throughout the organization—requires more than just sharing information bulletins. It requires the creation of forums for dialogue and interaction that can help span the cultural chasm between acquirer and acquiree.

As in any communication plan, there are four considerations: Audience, timing, mode, and message. For example, for one of its integrations, GE Capital's Private Label Credit Card business identified several distinct audiences: the senior managers of both organizations; the integration manager and his team; all of the employees of the acquired organization; all of GE Capital's employees; the customers, clients, and vendors of the combined company; the community; and the media. The appropriate time to communicate was identified for each audience—before the deal was closed, for instance, or at closing, or perhaps 60 days after the closing. And for each audience, the appropriate mode of communication was selected, ranging from newsletters and memos to videos to small-group huddles to town meetings and visits from management.

A fundamental message about GE Capital's culture underlay the entire communication effort—that at GE Capital, communication and involvement are valued and considered to be critical success factors; that GE Capital does not hide information from employees; that GE Capital wants to create a relationship of trust and open dialogue across all boundaries in the organization. That's why managers, and not professional communicators, are asked to take the lead in many aspects of the process—so that they will engage in dialogue with their employees, peers, customers, and others. At another level, messages about the course of the integration process are communicated by disseminating the 100–day plan itself, so that everyone has an opportunity to learn its broad outlines.

The assumption here is that the more people know about what is happening, the more they will be able to accept change and overcome their cultural and historical differences. But in GE Capital's experience, such intensive communication, even when combined with extensive integration planning, is sometimes not enough to bridge deep cultural gaps. A more direct approach to cultural integration may be needed as well.

Address the cultural issues head-on. Several years ago, as GE Capital began to make more acquisitions outside the United States, it became clear that a number of unrecognized cultural issues were getting in the way of fast and effective integration. Those issues were rooted in differences in corporate culture but were magnified and complicated by differences in national culture. For example, in some companies, deference to authority prevented managers from challenging, questioning, and thus enriching GE Capi-

It became clear that cultural issues were getting in the way of fast, effective integration.

tal's ideas about how to grow the new business. In countries with hierarchical social systems, this pattern of deference seemed to be even more apparent. In other settings, seemingly straightforward instructions were misinterpreted, not only because of language barriers but also because of assumptions about intentions. And in still other cases, GE Capital found that newly acquired leaders didn't comfortably accept the autonomy that comes along with empowerment.

To deal with those issues, GE Capital worked with a consulting firm to construct a systematic process of cross-cultural analysis, leading up to a structured three-day "cultural workout" session between GE Capital and the newly acquired management team. That process is now applied in most of GE Capital's acquisitions, especially when there is a significant non-U.S. component.

Here is how the process works. Using the results of focus groups and interviews with customers and employees, a computer-generated analysis is developed that plots the acquired company's culture on a scatter-gram across four dimensions: costs, technology, brands, and customers. The analysis also contrasts how employees see the company with the way customers see it. A similar survey is done for the GE Capital business.

Once the survey results are ready, the managers from both GE Capital and the acquired company meet for the three-day cultural workout. (If everything is on schedule, this meeting takes place at or close to the end of the first 100 days.) At that session, the data from the two companies are compared to highlight areas of convergence and difference. With a facilitator, participants go through the data and talk about why they think the results turned out the way they did. They talk about the history of their companies, the folklore, and the heroes that made them what they are. That leads to focused discussions about cultural differences and similarities and their implications for doing business—for instance, how to go to market, how much to focus on cost, or how concepts of authority differ.

By the third day of the session, participants shift their focus from the past to the future. Based on what has been accomplished in the first 100 days, they are asked two questions: Where do they want to take the company? and What kind of future do they want to create? That discussion results in a written outline of a new business plan for the acquired company, based on the goals that were established as part of the original deal, now augmented by the collective dreams and aspirations of the new management team. After the first 100 days, the stage is set for continuing the integration and development process over the next six months or more on the basis of a shared understanding of cultural differences and a concrete plan for bridging the gaps.

To move from the few to the many, cascade the integration process. Bridging cultural gaps with the acquired management team is critical to the integration process and almost always leads to a richer business plan to which more employees are committed. But in most cases, hundreds or even thousands of other people also need to be part of the process. How can that process of bridging cultures be spread beyond the management team?

A powerful way to integrate cultures is to assign short-term projects to yield quick results.

The results of the cultural workout can be widely shared and discussed through small-group meetings, videos, and other channels. That gives the wider employee population access to the same body of cultural data as the management team has—and the same opportunity to digest it and consider its implications for the integration. But a more powerful way to spread the cultural integration further is through action. Short-term projects that focus on achieving results quickly and include staff members from both GE Capital and the acquired company almost always serve to bridge the gap between cultures. In other words, the faster people from both companies are given opportunities to work together on important business issues, the faster integration will occur.

For example, in 1995, when GE Capital's Global Consumer Finance business acquired Minebea Financial, a Japanese financial-services company, the business leader commissioned a number of joint GCF-Minebea teams to accomplish critical business goals in the first 100 days. One team reduced the cost of materials through an initiative aimed at having the suppliers manage inventory. Another arranged for the sale of written-off receivables. Still another reduced the time it took to respond to customers' telephone calls from three minutes to ten seconds. As important as those results were, equally important was what the people from GCF and Minebea learned by working together. By achieving results quickly, everybody could immediately see the benefits of the acquisition—that more could be achieved together than could ever have been accomplished separately.

GE Capital also has been experimenting with other ways to help individuals deal with differences in national cultures. For example, an American assigned to lead a key function in India is individually coached by an external consultant who specializes in national cultures. The consultant can help the relocating manager understand in advance subtle, but critical differences in culture—the need for specific, rather than general, instructions, for example, or the importance of variations in attitudes toward class and gender, in the willingness to criticize others, or in the degree to which employees are expected to take initiative.

Finally, to introduce the GE Capital culture to high-potential leaders in those organizations newly acquired from outside the United States, the company has initiated a program called Capital University. In this program, selected middle managers are given 6- to 12-month assignments in a GE Capital business or head-office function in the United States. With their families, these managers learn not only about GE Capital but also about the national culture in which GE Capital is rooted. They, too, are coached individually by consultants about differences in national cultures.

A Work in Progress

For almost a decade, GE Capital's leaders have been thinking about how to make acquisition integration a core competence, and they have engaged hundreds of people in the effort. Starting in 1989, workout teams have mapped out the entire transaction process and have identified essential steps for integration. In 1992, GE Capital employed a "change acceleration" methodology to identify best integration practices and develop a set of model approaches. And since 1995, GE Capital has sponsored periodic conferences to refine those best practices, share tools and lessons, and discuss case studies of integration efforts currently in progress.

Today these lessons are available on-line to all GE

Capital business leaders over the company's intranet. There, too, are communication plans, 100–day plans, functional integration checklists, workshop agendas, consulting resources, and the like. A staff member from the corporate human-resources department keeps these materials up-to-date and assists in accessing them.

Despite this progress, acquisition integration remains an ongoing challenge for GE Capital. The structure of every acquisition is unique; each has a one-of-a-kind business strategy; each has its own personality and culture. No matter how many insights and models previous transactions generate, the next deal is always different, as much an art as a science. Therefore, any company that hopes to benefit from GE Capital's experience needs to accept at least one aspect of its culture—that competence is something never fully attained, that it is only the jumping-off point for an ever higher standard. Today, drawing from the lessons it has learned, GE Capital is better at acquisitions than it was last year. But next year, the goal is to be even better.

What It Takes to Be an Integration Manager

INTEGRATION MANAGERS MANAGE THE INTEGRATION PROCESS, not the business. To do so, they:

Facilitate and manage integration activities by

- Working closely with the managers of the acquired company to make its practices consistent with GE Capital's requirements and standards.

- Creating strategies to quickly communicate important information about the integration effort to employees.

- Helping the new company add functions that may not have existed before, such as risk management or quality improvement.

Help the acquired business understand GE Capital by

- Assisting managers of the newly acquired company as they navigate through the GE Capital system—explaining to a new finance manager in Taipei, for example, who reports to a business in Chicago, how to buy a personal computer through the GE purchasing network.

- Educating the new management team about GE Capital's business cycle; reviews; and such other processes as strategic planning, budgeting, and human resource assessments.

- Translating and explaining GE's and GE Capital's various acronyms.

- Helping managers of the acquired company understand GE Capital's culture and business customs.

- Helping managers of the acquired company understand both the fundamental and minor changes in their jobs. For example, a CFO accustomed to having full responsibility for tax and treasury accounting needs to be informed that CFOs in the GE Capital system don't usually cover that territory.

- Introducing GE Capital's business practices to the new company, including its "workout," "quality leadership," "change acceleration," and "management-education" programs.

Help GE Capital understand the acquired business by

- Making sure managers of the newly acquired company are not swamped with requests for information from GE Capital. A number of integration managers insist, for example, that all requests for information go through them so that they can sort through the important ones and allow the other managers to stay focused on the business.

- Briefing GE executives about the newly acquired company to help them understand why it works the way it does.

Originally published in January–February 1998
Reprint 98101

Capturing the Value of Supplementary Services

JAMES C. ANDERSON AND

JAMES A. NARUS

Executive Summary

VIRTUALLY ALL MANAGERS ARE AWARE that the key to winning in market after market today is tailoring one's offerings to the needs of each customer while maintaining low costs and prices. But most manufacturers have focused only on the products themselves, largely ignoring another element that differentiates a company's offerings and has a huge impact on costs and profits: services.

Instead of tailoring their packages of services to customers' individual needs, many suppliers simply add layers of services to their offerings. The authors have found that suppliers usually give customers more services than they want at prices that reflect neither their value to customers nor the cost of providing them. Many companies don't know which services customers with similar needs really want, nor do they understand which services should be part of a standard package and which can be offered as options. Most companies don't even know the cost of providing many of their services. And all too many let salespeople give away services to land a deal, even if those freebies reduce profitability.

But some companies are realizing that they can lower the cost of providing services and use them more effectively to meet customers' needs, gain more business, and enhance profits. From the authors' study of the best practices of those companies, they have developed a model for providing *flexible service offerings*, which they believe will help a wide range of manufacturing and service companies figure out how to reduce the number and cost of services they use to augment their core products, how to charge more for those services on average, and how to provide greater value to customers.

V IRTUALLY ALL MANAGERS ARE KEENLY AWARE that the key to winning in market after market today is excelling in tailoring one's offerings to the specific needs of each customer while still maintaining low costs and prices. In pursuit of those goals, suppliers have installed flexible manufacturing systems, created modular components that can be assembled in a wide variety of configurations, and designed platforms that can be shared by a family of products. But surprisingly, most manufacturers have focused only on the products themselves. They have largely ignored another element that plays a crucial role in differentiating a company's offerings and has a huge impact on costs and profits: services.

By services, we mean much more than technical problem solving, equipment installation, training, and maintenance. We also are talking about programs that help customers to design their products or reduce their costs as well as rebates or bonuses that influence how customers do business with a supplier. And we also include systems such as logistics management; electronic data interchange for placing orders and tracking their status; and expert systems that figure out, for example, which materials can deliver desired functional performance to customers.

Instead of tailoring their packages of services to customers' individual needs in order to win, retain, or increase the amount of their business, many suppliers simply add layer upon layer of services to their offerings. From our research, we have found that suppliers typically provide customers with more services than they want or need at prices that often reflect neither the value of those services to customers nor the cost of providing them. Many companies do not even know which services individual customers or groups of customers with similar needs really want. A surprising number don't really understand which services should be offered as a standard package accompanying either a product or a core service and which can be offered as options because individual customers value them so much that they will pay extra for them. Most companies do not even know the cost of providing many of their services. And all too many continue to let salespeople give away whatever services they think it will take to land a deal, even if those freebies dramatically reduce the profitability of the business.

But a relative handful of companies are beginning to recognize that they can reduce the cost of providing services *and* use services more effectively to meet customers' requirements, get more of their business, and enhance profits. To understand these emerging practices better, we conducted an extensive study. We organized four roundtable discussions with managers in a wide variety of industries in the Chicago, Illinois, and Charlotte, North Carolina, metropolitan areas, where we are located. We then conducted field studies of 22 large and medium-size U.S., European, and Japanese companies. All of them serve business-to-business markets—in other words, they supply institutions, governments, and other organizations, not the final consumer. These companies were in various stages of grappling with the problem, and only a handful—including Sonoco Products Company, Baxter International, ABB Asea Brown Boveri, and AKZO—had come close to developing and implementing a complete approach. But from the best practices of each company, we were able to develop a model for providing what we call *flexible service offerings*. This model, we believe, will enable a wide range of

Managers should analyze their services and decide which must be offered as standard and which can be offered as options.

manufacturing and service companies to figure out how to reduce the number and cost of services they use to augment their core products, how to charge more for those services on average, and how to provide greater value to customers.

No matter how painstakingly a company segments its market into groups of customers that need similar packages of products and services, one size will not fit all. Each customer will inevitably have some requirements not shared by others in the segment. Our research found that most suppliers either are not aware of this fact or have avoided dealing with its implications. Rather, they have provided "standard" packages of products and services designed to meet the needs of the "average" customer in each segment.

But companies that adopt our model can take advantage of this inevitable variation in customers' needs by building flexibility into their portfolio of services. Doing so entails constructing what companies such as ABB and Microsoft Corporation have dubbed *naked solutions* or *naked systems*. These are the bare-bones-minimum number of services uniformly valued by all customers in a given segment, which the supplier should strive to sell at the lowest possible price that will yield a profit. These naked solutions should then be "wrapped" with options—particular services valued by individual customers within the segment. Redeploying services in this manner will give suppliers greater latitude in pricing.

Creating **naked solutions** *for each customer segment allowed Apple Computer to lower costs.*

This approach enabled Sonoco's Industrial Products Division to customize its packages of products and services to meet more precisely the requirements of its spectrum of customers. Creating naked solutions for each customer segment from service modules allowed Apple Computer to achieve greater economies of scale and lower costs. ABB found that naked solutions enabled it to charge less for power equipment and heavy industrial equipment than it could for the standard package designed for the average customer. This approach helped it gain the business of companies that had spurned its products for lower-priced Japanese offerings. And once ABB won those companies and explained the value of its various optional services, many of these new customers then agreed to trade up by buying those services.

Perhaps the most important benefit of flexible service offerings is that they can provide suppliers with a powerful means of retaining and expanding business with their most valuable customers. That is exactly what Baxter Healthcare Corporation, a subsidiary of Baxter International, tried to do. It divided its hospital customers into two categories: strategic (those that have committed themselves in contracts to building a broad, long-term relationship with Baxter) and transactional (those that do business with Baxter on an order-by-order basis). Then Baxter focused its services on helping its strategic customers to improve *their* medical services and financial performance. Even the services offered only as options to strategic customers reflect this priority: they are carefully designed to provide value or savings that far exceed their cost.

Getting Started

A first step that a company should take to turn its services into flexible offerings is to inventory its supplementary services. Although that may seem obvious, many managers do not know all the services in their portfolios, which ones are being provided to which customers, and on what basis they are being provided. (A number of companies segment their markets but still offer much the same—if not exactly the same—services to most or even all of the segments.) Why is such ignorance so common? Because managers tend to spend the bulk of their time on their products or core services and

too little on understanding or keeping track of their supplementary services. This habit also helps explain the
lack of rhyme or reason in the way many companies we
studied charged customers for supplementary services.

All too often, salespeople are guilty of "fourth-quarter
habits": giving away optional services at the end of the
year to meet their sales quotas. Moreover, because salespeople tend to focus on the transaction and often don't
know how or why to say no to demands for free services,
they confuse customers' expectations about which services should be standard and which optional. Some
salespeople make certain options de facto standard by
always waiving the charges. For example, one textile
company in our study offered TQM-based cost-
reduction studies as an optional service. A company
review, however, showed that its principal customer
repeatedly received the service for free.

After compiling a complete inventory of supplementary services, a company should assess the value of each
service and the cost of providing it. Although it is virtually impossible to manage one's services strategically
without this information, remarkably few businesses try
to obtain it.

ASSESSING VALUE

Most companies rely solely on measures of customer
satisfaction instead of assessing the value of their services. Because the former identify customers' expectations and how well the supplier lives up to them, they do
serve a function. But their findings can be misleading,
and depending exclusively on those findings, instead of
measuring the value of services, can lead to serious
errors in judgment. For one thing, customers are

understandably happier when they receive services for free than when they have to pay for them. While giving away an ever greater number of services will undoubtedly increase customer satisfaction, it will also cause costs to soar and profits to shrink.

How do leading-edge companies measure value? Sonoco's Industrial Containers Division, which produces fiber and plastic drums, routinely conducts what it calls cost-in-use studies to document the incremental cost savings and thus the superior value a customer gains by using Sonoco products and services. Working together with customer managers, one of Sonoco's technical service managers performs a series of process-flow analyses outlining the customer's entire business operations and estimating their costs. Using those estimates, all the Sonoco employees involved with the account then brainstorm to come up with system solutions—for instance, a complete materials-handling system that includes just-in-time deliveries and drum recycling. Sonoco then gives the customer a variety of service alternatives together with estimates of the cost savings that each is likely to generate. In this way, the customer can make informed purchasing decisions based on the value of the proposed system solutions.

Relying solely on measures of customer satisfaction can lead to serious errors in judgment.

Baxter Corporate Consulting, which helps Baxter Healthcare's strategic hospital customers cut costs and improve quality, provides another way of measuring accurately how customers value services. Each proposal that the consulting unit submits to hospitals includes a set of mutually defined metrics for determining the value of the study to the client. As a condition for using the consulting unit, the client must agree to work with it to apply those metrics and document the results. Armed with this information, Baxter Corporate Consulting can then give other prospective clients a concrete idea of the benefits they will reap by using its services.

ASSESSING COSTS

Despite recent strides in the development and implementation of activity-based costing, we found that few companies use this tool to manage services. That is understandable. Existing activity-based-costing techniques have largely been applied to the measurement of manufacturing and product-related costs, and little work has been done to apply them to services. Managers at many companies rarely define concretely what constitutes a particular service and its various levels. For example, "technical problem solving" can run the gamut from a salesperson who tells a customer over the phone to use part A instead of part B to an engineering team that works for months with a customer to redesign a faulty manufacturing process. Because of this fuzzy definition, managers have difficulty tracking which customer got what service and allocating related costs.

Another reason so few companies apply activity-based costing to services is that accounting systems at many companies allow sales forces to foist service costs on other departments. A typical scenario: to close a deal, a sales representative promises an extraordinary level of service in the form of design assistance. Neither the customer nor the sales rep is booked for the service. Instead, the charges are buried in the fixed costs of the engineering department, which does the work for the customer, making customer service costs difficult, if not impossible, to determine.

A final reason why activity-based costing is rarely applied to services is that many companies are organized around products rather than around market segments or customers. As a result, they can readily break down costs on a product-by-product basis but cannot aggregate product and service costs on a segment-by-segment or customer-by-customer basis.

How do exemplary organizations deal with such problems? Consider what Van Den Bergh Foods Company, a manufacturer of food additives and seasonings, did. It began by more precisely defining its services and the levels it offered. It then gave its sales force responsibility for handling all minor services (like basic problem solving). Technical experts from departments such as customer service handled major services (like detailed technical problem solving). Today the sales representative and, in turn, a specific customer are charged for each project. At the beginning of each year, Van Den Bergh managers construct an annual plan for every customer that defines financial and volume targets and sets the levels of services. At the end of the year, they review those plans, examine service costs and account profitability, and recommend any necessary changes in service levels for the following year.

Managers of the industrial-coatings unit of Netherlands-based AKZO (now AKZO Nobel) successfully employed value assessment in conjunction with activity-based costing to make a poorly performing business solidly profitable. The effort began about ten years ago. Wondering whether the unit was providing more services than customers were paying for, AKZO managers developed activity-based-costing tools to analyze each customer's contribution to profits. Then, relying on an industrial engineering approach, they determined the value of each service offered. For example, managers quantified the value of sending an investigating engineer to analyze dust in a customer's paint line.

As a result of the study, the managers of the AKZO unit found that they were indeed providing more services than many customers were paying for. They also discovered that some of their services were of little value to customers. These findings helped the managers to target those industries and market segments where their products and services provided the greatest value to customers and thus held the greatest potential for profit. And using customer-contribution-to-profit measures to guide them, they then revamped the services they offered as well as their prices.

Managers should try to limit their standard packages to those services that are highly valued by all customers in a segment.

Estimating the value and cost of services is not always easy; the AKZO effort, for example, took two years. However, armed with such information, suppliers can move the focus of discussions with customers away from price to performance and meeting customers' requirements.

Formulating Flexible Service Offerings

In trying to make their companies' service offerings more flexible, managers might find it helpful to divide their services into three categories: existing standard services, existing optional services, and new services.

REEVALUATING STANDARD SERVICES

In constructing flexible service offerings, the overriding goal should be to limit the standard package to just those services that are highly valued by all the customers in a segment. How rudimentary this package should be will vary by market segment. Obviously, those "vanilla" services that most industry players supply in their standard packages must be retained. The challenge then becomes to reduce the cost of providing them to a level below the competition's without undermining their perceived value to customers. When companies reassess their standard packages, they inevitably will decide to eliminate some services (in other words, not offer them even as options) and recast others as options. Of course, they also may decide to add services to the standard package that were not included before.

In our study, we found that suppliers were far more reluctant to eliminate existing services than to add new ones. In particular, engineers and customer service employees who had designed and implemented services often fought attempts to eliminate them. Their pride of ownership or their obsession with the elegance rather than the practicality of the delivered service frequently thwarted pruning efforts. Salespeople used to throwing in services at the last minute to win bids also protested, fearing the cuts would hurt their ability to close deals and meet sales quotas.

For their part, managers universally insist that recasting a standard service as an option is one of the most difficult actions to take. What customer, they point out, wants to pay for something that once was free? And it is even harder, they say, when competitors continue to market the service as standard. Nowhere is this a more serious problem than in industries with high fixed costs, like commodity industrial chemicals and integrated steelmaking. In such industries, senior executives often hesitate to implement any scheme that may reduce sales for fear that such a drop will jeopardize their ability to operate their plants at a high enough rate to break even or make a profit. As a result, they routinely add services to maintain volume—and rarely eliminate them.

We found that suppliers used a variety of approaches when recasting standard services as options that add value. Many looked first to infrequently performed services that deliver value on occasion—like training, installation, and retrofitting. By marketing them as value-added options rather than simply dropping them, they retained business with customers that still valued them. This approach is also a litmus test for services that customers value but won't admit that they value because they want to continue getting them for free. Depending on the market response, those services can be retained as options or discontinued.

One specialty chemical company devised a clever way to make the overhaul of its standard package more palatable to customers. Along with specialty organic chemicals, it offered a variety of costly services, including laboratory support, field consulting, on-site testing, and educational seminars. It continued to offer the same variety of services but simply changed the level of those services available in its standard package. If a customer buys a minimum amount of the company's products each year, it receives "basic" levels of all the services as standard. If the customer wants a higher level of services, it can either increase its annual product purchases to a prespecified amount or pay extra.

As a prelude to recasting some previously standard field services as value-added options, a large computer company began listing a charge for them, which it then subtracted from the customer's invoice with the notation "Do not pay this." A letter accompanying the invoice stated that the company was pleased to have provided the services and gave an estimate of what they were worth—based on the rates charged by independent industry consultants. Positioning the services as extras gave the company the option of charging secondary customers in the future.

REEVALUATING OPTIONAL SERVICES

After reevaluating their companies' standard services, managers should turn their attention to existing optional services. If the cost of an optional service exceeds customers' willingness to pay for it, the service should be discontinued. Changes in technology, required expertise, or insurance risks can greatly reduce or even eliminate the value of optional services that at one time gave companies a competitive edge. Suppliers can sometimes help the handful of customers that still need those services (or discontinued standard services, for that matter) to obtain them from other companies.

As we mentioned, there are circumstances in which a supplier might want to add a previously optional service to its standard package—for example, when the product itself is a commodity that can be differentiated only by packaging it with services not offered by the competition. But it is easy to go overboard. Believing that the supplier with the most extensive set of services often gets the business, managers in such highly competitive markets are continually tempted to fold existing optional services (as well as new services) into the standard package. They should resist. Instead, they might, for example, offer a bare-bones-minimum standard package of services, cut the price for the product and the standard services, and then let customers buy the options they want.

Another alternative—one that Baxter Healthcare adopted—is to let customers buy the optional services wholly or in part with "bonus dollars." The more the customer concentrates its purchases with the supplier, the more bonus dollars it earns and the more services it can "purchase." Not only does this approach allow customers to tailor the supplier's services to their particular needs, it also reinforces the message that they do not have to pay for services they do not want,

Customers of Baxter Healthcare earn "bonus dollars," which they can use to buy optional services that fit their individual needs.

which they have to do with a totally bundled package. And to underscore the value of the services it offers, a supplier can promise to give customers cash for any unused bonus dollars at the end of their agreement—something Baxter Healthcare does.

We found that some exemplary companies chose to retain services as options and had interesting reasons for doing so. For example, although Sonoco's Industrial Products Division manufactures and markets fiber cores, around which such products as newsprint, yarns, and plastic films are wrapped, management considers the group to be a service business. The division's managers try to offer customers as many options as possible. Customers receive an extensive menu of services—ranging from warehousing to analyzing how efficiently or effectively they are using packaging—from which each can create the set of services it will receive. Each service is priced according to its value and all the costs associated with providing it. Sonoco managers say the opportunity to select service options has delighted customers.

ADDING NEW SERVICES

Of course, making the most of one's supplementary services is not just a matter of rethinking how existing services are packaged and priced. It also involves the way new services are added to the mix. Each addition can serve a variety of strategic ends.

For instance, shrewd suppliers often add new services to standard offerings to thwart the competition. The Industrial Division of Baxter Scientific Products deliberately seeks out new services that customers value and that Baxter can deliver better than the competition or at lower costs. By including a new service in the standard package, Baxter forces competitors to choose from two unpleasant alternatives: If they do not offer the service, Baxter can tout its unique service as an extra benefit of doing business with the company. If competitors try to match Baxter and offer the same service, they have to endure the trials and tribulations and higher costs of learning how to deliver it effectively.

Introducing new services as options allows companies such as R.R. Donnelley to assess how much customers value them.

Offering new services as options has its own strategic advantage: it enables suppliers to gauge market interest. For example, although the traditional business of R.R. Donnelley & Sons Company is printing, management believes that future growth lies in innovative services such as database management, consulting and training, three-dimensional pop-up ads, talking ads (print ads with a microchip that plays a message), direct marketing, layout systems, and mapping services. To test the demand for those services, Donnelley is offering them as options.

Sometimes adding new optional services entails no more than offering new levels of an existing standard service. Managers should analyze each service their company offers only at a single level to determine whether they can define alternate levels that would have different values for different customers. For example, even though their utility customers traditionally had equipment-maintenance contracts, the managers of ABB's power transformers business recognized that not all of them wanted the same level of maintenance service or valued the service the same way. So the managers decided to offer both a basic package and an extraordinary package. In addition, the utilities do not have to buy either package for all their transformers. Some of them simply tell ABB which transformers to check and then ask how much ABB will charge for providing just that service. Each service contract's price is based on ABB's experience in providing the different levels of service to customers.

Pricing the Offerings

As several of these examples suggest, flexible service offerings enable managers to be more adaptive and responsive in their pricing. This approach also helps them make sure pricing decisions support their strategy for each market segment.

Obviously, what a company chooses to do with its prices when it trims services from its standard package depends on the competitive conditions it faces in a given market segment. In a cutthroat market, for example, a supplier might lower its prices by the full amount of the cost of the discontinued services. In a less competitive market, where the players have more flexibility in their pricing decisions, a supplier might maintain its prices or lower them by less than the cost of the eliminated services.

When enhancing the standard offering with additional services, managers have several choices: they can raise the price by an amount equal to the cost of providing the service, raise it less than the cost of providing the service, or perhaps even raise it slightly higher to camouflage a price increase. Several suppliers in our study that were competing in relatively stable markets and whose priority was gaining market share chose not to change their prices; they wanted to use the added options to gain new business. Others, which were competing in markets where price-cutting was rife, added options to avoid having to cut prices. Still others opted to try to gain market share by lowering prices even as they expanded the standard package.

Offering services as options gives a manager a wider choice of pricing tactics. One is to show the charge for the option on an invoice and then subtract it for a specific reason (for example, initial-use discount). This approach makes it easier to keep track of service giveaways. Yet it gives the company the flexibility to respond quickly to specific situations—like the need to blunt a competitive inroad or to attract business in targeted new segments. Mitsubishi Electric Industrial Controls offers a proprietary software development tool as an option that it sometimes provides at no charge to win a new account. Mitsubishi also may initially offer a new customer a separate option—consulting services on how to use the tool—free of charge. But it charges for subsequent consulting.

What we are suggesting is that flexible pricing is a particularly desirable consequence of flexible service offerings. One company that certainly understands this connection is Microsoft. Faced with customers' requests for greater choice on the one hand and its own rising costs on the other, Microsoft created a number of flexible service offerings. Now customers can select from among four basic types of increasingly sophisticated technical support. They range from Fast Tips & Electronic Services (a 24-hour automated system) to Premier Support (custom consulting on highly specialized applications). Depending on the type of software purchased, which ranges from Desktop Applications (for example, Word or Excel) to Advanced Systems (for example, Windows NT), these services are either not offered, marketed as standard, or marketed as optional "for fee." Particularly interesting is Microsoft's practice of giving customers a choice of payment plans for each for-fee optional service. They can buy an annual contract. They can purchase "incident packs" that entitle them to receive technical support on a specific number of occasions. They can pay by the incident. Or they even can choose to be billed by the minute!

Creating Value Merchants

Few traditional sales forces know how to sell value. Recognizing this fact, several companies that have adopted the flexible approach to services revamped their sales-force philosophies and practices before introducing their updated service packages.

One that we mentioned already is Van Den Bergh Foods. Another is Allen-Bradley Company. Its Automation Group requires the costs of key services such as training, support, and application assistance to come out of someone's pocket: they must either be charged against sales or be reflected in the price the salesperson gets for the package. The group also charges customers for problem-solving assistance if it can show that they misused the product or did not maintain it properly. In addition, various functional areas within the Automation Group are charged for services. For instance, engineering is charged if a poorly designed product generates substantial warranty work.

Some leading-edge companies have also worked hard to provide their salespeople with the means to be more persuasive in explaining the value of their services to customers. Sonoco, which typically charges a premium for its products, provides its salespeople with *value-in-use* case studies. These studies help the salespeople demonstrate that Sonoco's products and services result in greater sales to end users and are more innovative and less costly than the competition's.

The Industrial Products Division's sales representatives also now have two ways of helping a given customer select the particular packages that it thinks will deliver the greatest value. As we noted earlier, the customer can choose from a detailed menu of Sonoco's products and services. Or if the customer prefers, the sales reps can assemble several tailored packages of products and services. Along with the prices of each proposed package, the sales reps provide a summary of how much money the customer can expect to save if it buys that package. Sonoco managers report that since they began offering such extensive choices, both sales volume and market share have increased.

But to make this kind of pitch, sales forces need much more information about the cost and profitability of services than most companies typically have entrusted to them. Only with this knowledge can they focus effectively on the accounts with the greatest profit potential.

Compensation also has to support the mission. By and large, people do what they are paid to do. Those in sales are no different. For this reason, companies that want to turn their salespeople into value merchants must tie their compensation to increasing long-term profitability and not just boosting this quarter's sales or profits.

That is what Sonoco's Consumer Products Division, which makes products such as fiber tubes, has done. It divided customers' accounts on a market-by-market basis and then gave small cross-functional teams responsibility for a portfolio of accounts. In essence, each team manages its own business. Each develops market plans, prepares budgets, and initiates improvements to products and services. Sales managers can earn up to 50% and salespeople up to 25% of their salaries in bonuses, which are based on account sales and improvements in operating profits, customer satisfaction, accounts receivable levels, and securing long-term single-source supply contracts.

Companies that want to turn salespeople into value merchants should tie their pay to increasing long-term profits.

It is especially important for senior management to guard against compensation schemes that reward salespeople for selling as many services as they can to a given customer. While this policy may initially boost a customer's contribution to profits—a measure of sales-force performance—it tends to undermine a supplier's credibility with its customers and hurt the business over the long term.

Many companies refrain from implementing flexible service offerings for fear that charging extra for optional services that had been standard will cause certain customers to walk. One way to allay such fears is to conduct a pilot test. Either add a new service and offer it as an option or pick one service from the standard package and make it an option for which customers have to pay a surcharge. Then see what happens.

But the experiences of companies such as MCI should allay such fears. MCI managers don't worry about all the accounts they might lose. They're too busy exploiting their ability to do a better job of meeting customers' individual needs at reasonable prices. Flexible service offerings, they say, have helped MCI to increase business significantly. Other suppliers, such as AKZO Nobel, say they are getting a higher return by focusing their resources on the customers that value them the most.

But implementing flexible service offerings requires developing that most-difficult-to-acquire skill: the ability to say no adroitly to some customers. Suppliers must be willing to say no to customers that want full-service packages at no-frills prices. Without this skill, flexible service offerings devolve to business as usual—"giving it away." Practiced deftly, this approach will give a company the reputation of being firm, consistent, and fair.

Originally published in January–February 1995
Reprint 95101

Exploiting the Virtual Value Chain

JEFFREY F. RAYPORT AND JOHN J. SVIOKLA

Executive Summary

EVERY BUSINESS TODAY COMPETES IN TWO WORLDS: a physical world of resources that managers can see and touch and a virtual world made of information. Executives must pay attention to how their companies create value in both arenas—the *marketplace* and the *marketspace*. But the processes for accomplishing this are not the same in the two worlds. Managers who understand how to master both can create and extract value in the most efficient and effective manner.

The stages involved in creating value in the physical world are often referred to as links in a value chain. The value chain is a model that describes a series of value-adding activities connecting a company's supply side with its demand side. By analyzing the stages of a value chain, managers have been able to redesign their internal and external processes to improve efficiency and effectiveness. However, the value chain model treats information as a supporting element of the value-adding process, not as a source of value itself.

To create value with information, managers must look to the marketspace. The value-adding processes that companies must employ to turn raw information into new marketspace services and products are unique to the information world. In other words, the value-adding steps are *virtual* in that they are performed through and with information. Creating value in any stage of a virtual value chain involves a sequence of five activities: gathering, organizing, selecting, synthesizing, and distributing information. Just as someone takes raw material and refines it into something useful, so a manager today collects raw information and adds value through these five steps.

EVERY BUSINESS TODAY COMPETES IN TWO WORLDS: a physical world of resources that managers can see and touch and a virtual world made of information. The latter has given rise to the world of electronic commerce, a new locus of value creation. We have referred to this new information world as the *marketspace* to distinguish it from the physical world of the *marketplace*. (See "Managing in the Marketspace," HBR November–December 1994.) A few examples illustrate the distinction. When consumers use answering machines to store their phone messages, they are using objects made and sold in the physical world, but when they purchase electronic answering services from their local phone companies, they are utilizing the marketspace—a virtual realm

where products and services exist as digital information and can be delivered through information-based
channels. Banks provide services to customers at
branch offices in the marketplace as well as electronic
on-line services to customers in the marketspace; airlines sell passenger tickets in both the "place" and the
"space"; and fast-food outlets take orders over the
counter at restaurants and increasingly through touch
screens connected to computers.

Executives must pay attention to how their companies create value in both the physical world and the virtual world. But the processes for creating value are not
the same in the two worlds.
To create and extract By understanding the differ-
value with information, ences and the interplay
managers must turn between the value-adding
to the virtual world of processes of the physical
the marketspace. world and those of the information world, senior man-
agers can see more clearly and comprehensively the
strategic issues facing their organizations. Managing
two interacting value-adding processes in the two mutually dependent realms poses new conceptual and tactical
challenges. Those who understand how to master both
can create and extract value in the most efficient and
effective manner.

Academics, consultants, and managers have long
described the process of creating value in the physical
world, often referring to the stages involved as links in a
"value chain." The value chain is a model that describes
a series of value-adding activities connecting a company's supply side (raw materials, inbound logistics, and
production processes) with its demand side (outbound
logistics, marketing, and sales). By analyzing the stages

of a value chain, managers have been able to redesign their internal and external processes to improve efficiency and effectiveness.

The value chain model treats information as a supporting element of the value-adding process, not as a source of value itself. For instance, managers often use information that they capture on inventory, production, or logistics to help monitor or control those processes, but they rarely use information itself to create new value for the customer. However, Federal Express Corporation recently did just that by allowing customers to track packages through the company's World Wide Web site on the Internet. Now customers can locate a package in transit by connecting on-line to the FedEx site and entering the airbill number. After the package has been delivered, they can even identify the name of the person who signed for it. Although FedEx provides this service for free, it has created added value for the customer— and thus increased loyalty—in a fiercely competitive market.

To create value with information, managers must look to the marketspace. Although the value chain of the space can mirror that of the place—buyers and sellers can transfer funds over electronic networks just as they might exchange cold, hard cash—the value-adding processes that companies must employ to turn raw information into new marketspace services and products are unique to the information world. In other words, the value-adding steps are *virtual* in that they are performed through and with information. Creating value in any stage of a virtual value chain involves a sequence of five activities: gathering, organizing, selecting, synthesizing, and distributing information. Just as someone takes raw material and refines it into something useful—as in the sequence of tasks involved in assembling an automobile on a production line—so a manager today collects raw information and adds value through these steps.

Adapting to a Virtual World

An examination of Geffen Records, a unit of MCA's music division, illustrates the use of information to create value. The traditional product of a major record label such as Geffen is a package of prerecorded music captured on an audiocassette or compact disc. The product is the end point of a set of value-adding processes that occur in the physical world. Those processes include discovering new musicians, screening them for potential marketability, recording their work in a studio, editing and selecting their music, creating master tapes, producing CDs or cassettes, and finally packaging, promoting, and distributing the products.

Increasingly, new competitors for Geffen's business are emerging in the marketspace. These entrants are viable because of the new economics of doing business in the world of information. For example, groups such as the Internet Underground Music Archive (IUMA) are posting digital audio tracks from unknown artists on the network, potentially subverting the role that record labels play. Today's technology allows musicians to record and edit material inexpensively themselves, and to distribute and promote it over networks such as the World Wide Web or commercial on-line services. They also can test consumers' reactions to their music, build an audience for their recorded performances, and distribute their products entirely in the marketspace.

The point here is simple: Bringing music to market can sometimes be done faster, better, and less expensively in the marketspace. Hence the challenge for Geffen. The company has a site on the World Wide Web devoted to the label's bands and uses it to distribute digital audio and video samples and to provide information about the bands' tours. The Web page has become Geffen's showroom in the marketspace and a potential new retail channel. It is also an information mirror of an activity that traditionally has occurred in the physical world—a stage in a virtual value chain that parallels a stage in a physical value chain.

In addition to using its own Web page, Geffen could search for new talent at IUMA's home site rather than audition bands in a studio, or edit and modify music on a computer rather than record take after take with a band to create one suitable version for the master tape. Each activity is a stage in a virtual value chain that occurs through and with information and mirrors a stage in the physical world.

To truly exploit the virtual value chain, however, Geffen's managers might go further by applying the generic value-adding steps of the marketspace to the information the company collects at every stage of the physical chain, thereby creating new value for customers. For example, they might utilize the digital information captured during a band's practice sessions by inviting fans to sit in the studio on the Internet. They might also allow fans to listen as engineers edit the material or to electronically download interviews with a band's members before they are published or distributed more widely. In the physical value chain, information collected in the studio or during editing has value to the extent that it enables Geffen to produce and sell CDs more efficiently; in the virtual world, it is a potential source of new revenue. Moreover, that information presents opportunities to develop new relationships with customers at very low cost—for instance, a customer not interested in a new compact disc by the Rolling Stones may nevertheless pay to sit in on a chat session with them in the Internet's Voodoo Lounge.

Like most companies, Geffen must play both in the place and in the space. The company's managers must continue to oversee a physical value chain—making and selling CDs—but they must also build and exploit a virtual value chain. We have studied scores of companies in a variety of industries attempting to do business in both the place and the space and have found that organizations making money in the information realm successfully exploit both of their value chains. Rather than managing one series of value-adding processes, they are actually managing two. The economic logic of the two chains is different: A conventional understanding of the economies of scale and scope does not apply to the virtual value chain (VVC) in the same way as it does to the physical value chain (PVC). Moreover, the two chains must be managed distinctly but also in concert.

We have observed that companies adopt value-adding information processes in three stages. In the first stage, *visibility*, companies acquire an ability to "see" physical operations more effectively through information. At this stage, managers use large-scale information technology systems to coordinate activities in their physical value chains and in the process lay the foundation for a virtual value chain. (See the chart "Building the Virtual Value Chain.") In the second stage, *mirroring capability*, companies substitute virtual activities for physical ones; they begin to create a parallel value chain in the marketspace. Finally, businesses use information to establish *new customer relationships*. At this third stage, managers draw on the flow of information in their virtual value chain to deliver value to customers in new ways. In effect, they apply the generic value-adding activities to their virtual value chain and thereby exploit what we call the *value matrix*.

As companies move into the information world to perform value-adding steps, the potential for top-line growth increases. Each of the three stages represents considerable opportunity for managers.

Visibility

During the last 30 years, many companies have invested in technology systems to enable managers to coordinate, measure, and sometimes control business processes. The information collected by these systems about steps in the value chain has helped managers to plan, execute, and evaluate results with greater precision and speed. In other words, information technology has allowed managers to see their operations more effectively through the information world. In recent years, managers have been able to gain access to the information generated in the course of traditional operating activities, and that

---

Building the Virtual Value Chain

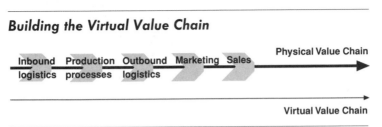

When companies integrate the information they capture during stages of the value chain from inbound logistics and production through sales and marketing—they construct an information underlay of the business. This integrated information provides managers with the ability to "see" their value chains from end to end.

information helps them see their physical value chains as an integrated system rather than as a set of discrete though related activities. In this way, they can gain new insight into managing the value chain as a whole rather than as a collection of parts.

Companies such as FedEx, Wal-Mart, and Frito-Lay have transformed this kind of visibility into competitive advantage. The successful use of world-class information systems by each of these companies is now common knowledge, but consider one example—Frito-Lay—from the perspective of the marketspace. Frito's achievement with its widely publicized "information revolution" initiative illustrates the necessary first steps companies must take if they are to establish and then exploit their virtual value chains.

Underlying the manufacture and distribution of a variety of Frito-brand snack foods is an efficient information system that gives managers the ability to visualize nearly every element of the company's value chain as part of an integrated whole. It is a central nervous system within the business that integrates marketing, sales, manufacturing, logistics, and finance; it also provides managers with information on suppliers, customers, and competitors.

Frito's employees in the field collect information on the sales of products daily, store by store across the nation, and feed it electronically to the company. The employees also collect information about the sales and promotions of competing products or about new products launched by competitors in select locations. By combining this field data with information from each stage of the value chain, Frito's managers can better determine levels of inbound supplies of raw materials, allocate the company's manufacturing activity across available production capacity, and plan truck routing for the most efficient coverage of market areas. The company's ability to target local demand patterns with just the right sales promotion means that it can continuously optimize margin in the face of inventory risk. In short, Frito can use information to see and react to activities along its physical value chain. The company executes actions in the marketplace while it monitors and coordinates those actions in the marketspace.

Mirroring Capability

Once companies have established the necessary infrastructure for visibility, they can do more than just monitor value-adding steps. They can begin to manage operations or even to implement value-adding steps in the marketspace—faster, better, with more flexibility, and at lower cost. In other words, managers can begin to ask, What are we doing now in the place, and what could we do more efficiently or more effectively in the space? What value-adding steps currently performed in the physical value chain might be shifted to the mirror world of the virtual value chain? When companies move activities from the place to the space, they begin to create a virtual value chain that parallels but improves on the physical value chain. (See "Exploiting the Virtual Value Chain.")

Executives at Ford Motor Company engaged in such work during the past decade as the company aggressively adopted videoconferencing and CAD/CAM technologies. When Ford developed its "global car" (marketed in North America as the Contour sedan), the automaker moved one key element of its physical value chain—product development—into the marketspace. Ford intended to create a car that would incorporate its

best engineering, design, and marketing talent worldwide while also bringing to bear a vision of how a single
car design could appeal at once to all major world markets. To gain leverage
from its substantial
investments in
marketspace-enabling
technology systems,
Ford brought manage-
rial talent from around the world together in the marketspace. Rather than creating national product teams
or convening elaborate design summits, Ford established a *virtual* work team to develop the car. In this
way, it extracted the best talent and the broadest vision
it could muster.

*Managers can begin to ask,
What could we do more
efficiently or effectively in
the marketspace?*

By moving product development from the place to the
space, Ford's managers did more than perform tasks in
an information-defined world that were traditionally
accomplished through physical actions. In the virtual
world, the design team could transcend the limitations of
time and space that characterize management in the
physical world. They built and tested prototypes in a

Exploiting the Virtual Value Chain

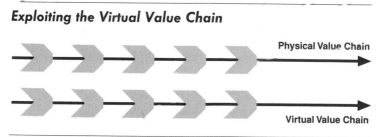

With an integrated information underlay in place, companies can begin to perform value-adding
activities more efficiently and effectively through and with information. In other words, these
information-based activities mirror steps in the physical value chain. When companies move a number of value-adding activities from the marketplace to the marketspace, they exploit a virtual value
chain.

simulated computer environment and shared the designs and data with colleagues over a computer network, 24 hours a day, around the world. In the virtual world of information, they established common global specifications for manufacturing, integrated component systems centrally, and even drew suppliers into the design process. Ford thus performed critical value-adding steps not on the PVC but on the VVC—in other words, in a world that mirrored traditional managerial realities.

With such a complete information-based representation of the product, everyone on the team could see the project holistically in the mirror world. The goal: a global car with global appeal. The virtual value chain made a much more integrated process possible. The marketing challenge of getting customers to buy the Contour remains.

Managers at the Boeing Company took their exploitation of the mirror world one step further. A few years ago, they redesigned the engine housing for a new model of the 737 airplane. Previously, Boeing and other airplane manufacturers would design airframes by developing physical prototypes, testing them in wind tunnels to gauge the flow of air over their contours, and then repeating the process through multiple iterations. When Boeing addressed the question of how to create a new engine to improve the performance of its existing 737 airframe design, it turned not to wind tunnels but to a synthetic environment—a mirror world made of information. Boeing engineers developed the prototype as a virtual product that incorporated relevant laws of physics and materials sciences and enabled the company to test an evolving computer-simulated model in a virtual wind tunnel. As a result, engineers could test many more designs at dramatically lower costs and with much greater speed. The outcome was a teardrop shape for the engine housing that stunned the aerospace world. Why? Because only a process that could endlessly test different possibilities at near-zero incremental cost per synthetic prototype could give rise to a product concept that was outside the bounds of conventional thinking. By moving elements of the PVC—R&D, product design, prototyping, and product testing—to the mirror world of the VVC, Boeing succeeded in shattering a dominant paradigm of engine design and delivered a product that easily outperformed the competition, a feat that had proved impossible in 20 years of wind-tunnel testing.

Every manager knows that staying competitive today depends on achieving higher levels of performance for customers while incurring lower costs in R&D and production. Traditionally, companies have gotten more for less by exploiting vast economies of scale in production while focusing on raising levels of quality. Japanese automakers such as Toyota have successfully pursued that strategy, delivering highly differentiated products at the lowest possible costs. When scale economies do not apply, as in many service-sector businesses, managers seeking better performance at lower cost can tap the mirror world, in which the economics are altogether different. On the VVC, companies may find dramatic low-cost approaches to delivering extraordinarily high-value results to customers.

New Customer Relationships

Ultimately, however, companies must do more than create value in the space: They also must extract value from it. They can often do so by establishing space-based relationships with customers.

Once companies become adept at managing their value-adding activities across the parallel value chains, they are ready to develop these new relationships. In the world of high technology, examples of building customer relationships on the VVC abound. Today thousands of companies have established sites on the World Wide Web to advertise products or elicit comments from customers. Some companies have gone further and have actually automated the interface with the customer, thus identifying and fulfilling customers' desires at lower cost. Digital Equipment Corporation, making a comeback from its slump in the late 1980s, has developed a new channel for serving customers on the Internet. DEC's World Wide Web site allows prospective customers to use a personal computer to contact sales representatives, search for products and services, review the specifications of DEC equipment, and actually take a DEC machine for a "test drive." Similarly, Oracle Corporation, a data-base software maker, now distributes a new product over the Internet as well as through physical channels. These companies are joining the burgeoning ranks of major high-tech firms in the business-to-business sector that have become Internet marketers; the group includes GE Plastics, Sun Microsystems, and Silicon Graphics, all of which use the Web to establish and maintain relationships with selected accounts.

Once companies can manage value-adding activities across both chains, they can develop new customer relationships.

Other companies view their challenge as that of managing each individual customer relationship in both the marketspace and the marketplace. Those that succeed have an opportunity to reinvent the core value proposition of a business, even an entire industry. One extraordinary example of success in this regard is United Services Automobile Association, which has truly maximized its opportunities to deliver value to customers in both the space and the place and has thereby become a world-class competitor.

USAA began as an insurance company. Over time, it has used its information systems—installed to automate its core business, insurance sales and underwriting—to capture significant amounts of information about customers, both individually and in aggregate. USAA integrated information about customers and distributed it throughout the company so that employees are ready to provide products, services, and advice anytime a customer contacts the company. Having made this investment in visibility, USAA found that among other things it could prepare customer risk profiles and customize policies on the VVC. Looking at the flow of information harvested along its VVC, USAA's managers invented business lines targeted to specific customers' needs, such as insurance for boat owners.

But USAA also used its growing expertise with information to create new value for customers in ways that had little or nothing to do with insurance. For example, the company went one step further for the boat owners: It designed financing packages for purchasing boats. In fact, USAA now offers a wide range of financial products as well as shopping services for everything from jewelry to cars. Further, when a customer calls in with a theft claim, the company can offer to send a check or to replace the stolen item. (Many customers opt for the latter because it involves less work and solves their problem.)

By aggregating demand statistics and likely loss ratios, USAA has become a smart buyer for its loyal customer base, getting discount prices through high-volume purchases and passing some or all of the savings along to the customer. Today USAA is one of the largest direct merchandisers in the country, shipping real goods along its PVC as directed by the sensing capabilities of its VVC. USAA does not actually manufacture anything. Rather, it is a trusted intermediary between the demand it senses and the supply it sources.

Although USAA's "product line" is eclectic, it represents a logical, cost-effective, and profitable progression of new business ventures, all of which are underwritten by the information about customers captured in the company's virtual value chain. (Management of that information has become USAA's central activity.) Through clever integration of the information harvested along the VVC and through a PVC that delivers goods and services, USAA creates new value for customers by serving a broader set of their needs.

The Value Matrix

The new relationships that companies such as USAA are developing with customers spring from a matrix of value opportunities. Each stage of the virtual value chain—as a mirror of the physical value chain—allows for many new extracts from the flow of information, and each extract could constitute a new product or service. If managers want to pursue any of these opportunities, they need to put into place processes to gather the information, organize it for the customer, select what's valuable, package (or synthesize) it, and distribute it—the five value-adding steps unique to the information world. In effect, these value-adding steps, in conjunction with the virtual value chain, make up a value matrix that allows companies to identify customers' desires more effectively and fulfill them more efficiently. (See the chart "Value Matrix: Building Relationships.") For instance, when an automobile manufacturer can shift its R&D activities from the PVC to the VVC, it becomes possible for the company to exploit the matrix by engaging customers in the new-product-development process even if they are located around the world. The company could gather, organize, select, synthesize, and distribute design information drawn from the R&D process to create a computer simulation for customers, who could then enter the virtual design space and give feedback—which in turn could be used to add value in the unfolding design of the vehicle.

Moreover, the information can be turned into new spin-off products: Digitally captured product designs can become the basis for personal-computer-based or television-based multimedia software, such as the Lamborghini driving game, a software package now on the market. While the information used in such products

Value Matrix: Building Relationships

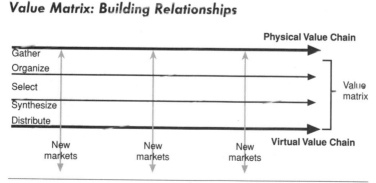

Companies create new markets and new relationships with existing markets by applying the five generic value-adding steps of the information world to each activity in the virtual value chain. They create a value matrix.

also aids physical processes and feeds into a physical end point—an automobile, a compact disc, an insurance policy—it is also the raw material for new kinds of value.

The newspaper industry is another example of how such processes can be shifted from the place to the space. Executives can apply the five value-adding steps to each link of the virtual value chain to envision a matrix of opportunities for creating value. For instance, drawing from the information used to support reporting and editing, newspapers could provide information packets to readers with audio files of reporters' interviews, images from their notebooks, photos that did not make it into the paper, and even editors' comments about early drafts of stories. The value matrix guides managers as they consider how to establish the processes necessary to exploit new opportunities.

Each extract from the flow of information along the virtual value chain could constitute a new product or service.

By thinking boldly about the integration of place and space, executives may be able to create valuable digital assets that, in turn, could change the competitive dynamics of industries. Consider Image Technology International (recently acquired by MCI Communications Corporation), a company that has entered the imaging market with an entirely digital approach to the capture, organization, selection, manipulation, and distribution of photographic images.

By using digital code as its raw material rather than chemicals as in traditional photography, Image can offer higher value to its customers in a number of ways. First, the company offers lower-cost prepress services. The cost of a high-quality industrial photo for a catalog is

$150 to $250 or more when captured on photographic film. The output of a chemical-based photo is limited: The incremental costs of using the image captured for the catalog in an additional product—such as a follow-on brochure—start at $15 and go up from there. In the world of digital code, the image (captured on a digital camera) costs half as much to create because of the photographer's increased productivity, the avoidance of chemical processing, improved image quality, and efficiencies of storage and manipulation.

Second, Image Technology can manipulate and reuse a digital photo in several different ways to allow businesses to communicate with their customers in either the marketplace or the marketspace. For instance, using specially designed software, the company can incorporate an image on acetate film or a digital press; both are used in printing promotional flyers. The same image can be directed to a photocopier to create a black-and-white or color copy of the same image for distribution of handbills announcing a sale. Image can manipulate a digital photo (which the company can organize in a database with other relevant data, such as the price of the object photographed and a text description of it) so that customers can use it in CD-ROM catalogs, videos, or on-line services. In short, by exploiting a virtual value chain the company can capture an image more efficiently and transform that image so that it can be used in many different physical processes—from dye transfer to photocopier to video—and virtual processes. Image can create an asset that has tremendous economies of scale and scope.

For example, consider one of the vertical markets Image competes in: the hardlines industry—the industry that makes, distributes, and sells hardware. Any business in the industry can use Image's preproduction technology to publish product images and data less expensively. A local hardware store can draw on Image's database of hammers, screwdrivers, and other products to create a newspaper flyer conventionally with pictures, halftones, and pasteup—or digitally, using Image's picture-processing software. A large distributor that wants to create a major catalog of product lines can do so less expensively, faster, and more flexibly using information-based services and products from Image. Whereas once the process of creating a catalog required tens of thousands of photos and months of layout work, Image can create a database of images and text for a customer far more quickly. Subsequent catalogs, drawing from the same digital asset, can be prepared for publication in just days, even if the distributor drops several items from the list and changes the price of many others or adds a broad range of hammers with different handle colors. Image can manipulate the size of images, reshuffle their order, and change text or even colors far more easily in the space than in the place.

In the process of helping hardline industry businesses to reduce the cost of communicating with their customers, Image is amassing a huge database of photos that will provide it with a dominant position in the industry. If Image's database can contain an industrial-grade picture of almost every piece of hardware in existence, why would any player in the hardlines channel—manufacturer, distributor, or retailer—go to another source or shoot a picture that was already available in physical and virtual form? (Pursuing the same logic, Bill Gates and other pioneers of electronic commerce are quickly buying up electronic rights to works of art and many other objects.)

To anyone who views Image's operations strictly as an information-based parallel to the traditional chemical process, the company's value chain merely looks far more efficient than other companies' physical value chains. However, considering how value is added in the information world, Image has in fact reinvented the business model for the capture and display of images. To create and process a photo, Image gathers information (finds subjects and takes photographs); organizes information (creates the photo database); selects information (chooses images to produce from the database); synthesizes information (processes images for different media); and distributes information (outputs images to relevant platforms). Image does not make and process the digital equivalent of photographic film and ancillary products. It parlays its digital assets across many forms, from newsprint to catalogs to videos. That is, by thinking in terms of a virtual value chain *and* a physical value chain, the company's managers look at far more opportunities for creating and extracting value than they would have by considering the business exclusively from the point of view of a traditional physical value chain. Thinking about a business in terms of its value matrix can allow managers to go beyond changing the rules of the game: They can reinvent an industry.

Companies that create value with digital assets may be able to reharvest them in an infinite number of transactions.

Such thinking is springing up around the world as new ways of creating and extracting value in the marketspace become clear. For example, the China Internet Company, backed by the Xinhua News Agency, will roll out a network of Internet sites for 40 industrial cities in

China before the end of 1995. On this network will be multimedia documents that describe a wide range of products, from toys to towels to auto parts. The China Internet Company will also provide a complete catalog of Chinese laws pertaining to trade and export, a translation service, and news. Because the Chinese do not have an adequate physical infrastructure for information about exports, they hope to create a virtual platform *first*. This new information infrastructure could easily become the basis for a whole new transaction and communications infrastructure into and out of China. After all, unlike a company entering the physical marketplace, the China Internet Company will have global reach the very instant it goes on-line.

Implications for Management

What all this means for managers is that they must consciously focus on the principles that guide value creation and extraction across the two value chains separately and in combination. These two value-adding processes are fundamentally different. The physical value chain is composed of a linear sequence of activities with defined points of input and output; in Geffen's case, it runs from locating new bands to manufacturing and distributing CDs of a band's music. By contrast, the virtual value chain is nonlinear—a matrix of potential inputs and outputs that can be accessed and distributed

In the marketspace, many of the business axioms that have guided managers don't apply.

through a wide variety of channels. USAA can meet customers' needs wherever and however they are manifested. Image can deliver images and data on a wide variety of platforms and across a wide variety of distribution infrastructures. The China Internet Company may perform similar functions for an entire burgeoning national economy.

How can we make sense of this new realm of activity—the information space that allows for the creation of a virtual value chain and the exploitation of a value matrix? To succeed in this new economic environment, executives must understand the differences between value creation and extraction in the marketplace and in the marketspace; they must manage both effectively and in concert. More specifically, a company's executives must embrace an updated set of guiding principles because in the marketspace many of the business axioms that have guided managers no longer apply. We offer five new principles here.

THE LAW OF DIGITAL ASSETS

Digital assets, unlike physical ones, are not used up in their consumption. Companies that create value with digital assets may be able to reharvest them through a potentially infinite number of transactions, thus changing the competitive dynamics of their industries. For example, when Image Technology gathers and organizes a million images of hardware, it will have the dominant digital asset in that industry. Companies using traditional chemical-based processes will have a difficult time competing with Image because the variable cost of creating value using digital-information assets is zero or close to it. Therefore providers of products or services that must price according to the traditional variable-cost model—based on the consumption of the underlying materials—will have a tough time competing against companies that, by exploiting their virtual value chains, can price aggressively and still make margin.

NEW ECONOMIES OF SCALE

The virtual value chain redefines economies of scale, allowing small companies to achieve low unit costs for products and services in markets dominated by big companies. The U.S. Postal Service, which views the world according to an industrial paradigm, could never afford to build a post office in every one of the nation's homes. But FedEx has done exactly that in the marketspace by allowing individuals with access to the Internet to track packages through the company's site on the World Wide Web. (Customers can also request software from FedEx that allows them not only to track their parcels but also to view at any time the entire history of their transactions with FedEx.) The new economies of scale make it possible for FedEx to provide what are, in effect, ministorefronts to each and every customer, whether millions of users request the service at any given moment or just one.

NEW ECONOMIES OF SCOPE

In the marketspace, businesses can redefine economies of scope by drawing on a single set of digital assets to provide value across many different and disparate markets. USAA dominates the insurance market for military officers with a 97% segment share, a scale of operations built on direct marketing. Now, through the new customer relationships made possible by its digital assets (the information USAA collected about its customers), the company is expanding its scope. Using its virtual value chain, USAA can coordinate across markets and provide a broader line of high-quality products and services.

TRANSACTION-COST COMPRESSION

Transaction costs along the VVC are lower than their counterparts on the PVC, and they continue to decline sharply as the processing capacity per unit of cost for microprocessors doubles every 18 months. In the 1960s, it cost about $1 to keep information about an individual customer. Today it costs less than one cent per customer. Lower transaction costs allow companies to control and track information that would have been too costly to capture and process just a few years ago. For instance, lower transaction costs made it possible for Frito to monitor its value chain from shipments of corn to in-store inventory.

REBALANCING SUPPLY AND DEMAND

Taken together, these four axioms combine to create a fifth: The world of business increasingly demands a shift from supply-side to demand-side thinking. As companies gather, organize, select, synthesize, and distribute information in the marketspace while managing raw and manufactured goods in the marketplace, they have the opportunity to "sense and respond" to customers' desires rather than simply to make and sell products and services. (See "Managing by Wire," by Stephan H. Haeckel and Richard L. Nolan, HBR September–October 1993.) USAA senses a demand in its customer base and then connects that demand to a source of supply. In today's world of overcapacity, in which demand, not supply, is scarce, managers must increasingly look to demand-side strategies.

Senior managers must evaluate their business—its strengths and weaknesses, its opportunities and risks—along the value chains of both worlds, virtual and physical. Today events in either can make or break a business.

Originally published in November–December 1995
Reprint 95610

About the Contributors

JAMES C. ANDERSON is the William L. Ford Distinguished Professor of Marketing and Wholesale Distribution, and Professor of Behavioral Science in Management, J. L. Kellogg Graduate School of Management, Northwestern University. His research interests are in working relationships between firms in business markets and measurement techniques for assessing the value of market offerings. His articles have appeared in *Harvard Business Review, Journal of Marketing, Journal of Marketing Research, Psychological Bulletin,* and *Psychometrika,* among others. He has been vice president of the Business Marketing Division of the American Marketing Association and is a fellow of the American Psychological Association. He has consulted and provided seminars for a number of firms in North America and Europe.

PATRICIA L. ANSLINGER is a principal in McKinsey & Company's New York Office and leads the firm's Corporate Finance and Acquisitions Practice. She earned her MBA from Anderson Graduate School of Management. She has published in *Directors & Boards, Harvard Business Review,* and *McKinsey Quarterly.*

RONALD N. ASHKENAS is a business author and managing partner of the management consulting firm, Robert H. Schaffer & Associates. The firm is well known for its results-focused approach, which helps organizations rapidly achieve major gains in productivity, quality, service, and product development in ways that strengthen management's ability to sustain progress. "Making the Deal Real" is Mr. Ashkenas's second *Harvard Business Review* article; his articles on organizational change have been widely published in many other leading business journals. He is the lead author of *The Boundaryless Organization: Breaking the Chains of Organizational Structure* (Jossey-Bass, 1995).

BENJAMIN BURNETT is vice president of The Boston Consulting Group (BCG) in Chicago. He is a member of BCG's Consumer Goods and Retail and Financial Services Practice Groups. Mr. Burnett has worked with a number of packaged goods and retail clients in developing corporate strategies, building brands, driving trade execution, conducting competitive analyses, and driving innovation and growth. In particular, he has helped clients identify sources of growth through deeper consumer understanding.

THOMAS E. COPELAND is director of financial services at McKinsey & Company in New York. Prior to joining McKinsey in 1987, he was a professor of finance at UCLA. Mr. Copeland has published over 40 articles and four books translated into nine languages. He is a member of the editorial board of Financial Management, and chairman of the practitioner board of directors. He is currently an adjunct professor of finance at New York University.

ARIE DE GEUS worked for the Royal Dutch/Shell Group for 38 years. Since his retirement, he has advised many government and private institutions and has lectured throughout the world, as well as accepting appointments as visiting fellow at London Business School and as a board member of both the Organizational Learning Center at MIT and the Nijenrode Learning Center in The Netherlands. His publications include an influential article entitled "Planning as Learning" in *Harvard Business Review*, a lecture entitled "Companies, What Are They?" published by the Royal Society of Arts, London (1995), and the best-selling business book entitled *The Living Company* (HBS Press, 1997).

LAWRENCE J. DEMONACO is the vice president of Global Human Resources at GE Capital Services, where he has worked on more than 100 acquisitions. He began his career in GE in the Employee Relations Management Program in 1969 at the Transportation Systems Business. Including an assignment in plastics, the first 10 years of his career were spent in a variety of union relations assignments. Mr. DeMonaco worked at the Engineered Materials Group in Columbus, Ohio, before moving to GE Capital in Stamford, Connecticut, in 1987.

SUZANNE C. FRANCIS is a senior partner of Robert H. Schaffer & Associates (RHS&A). Since joining the firm she has played a lead role with a number of its major clients. Over the past five years she has worked with GE Capital to develop and apply its acquisition integration process. Prior to joining RHS&A, Ms. Francis worked for Xerox as well as other corporate, government, and nonprofit organizations.

W. CHAN KIM is The Boston Consulting Group Bruce D. Henderson Chair Professor of Strategy and International Management at INSEAD. Prior to joining INSEAD, he was a professor at the University of Michigan Business School. He has published numerous articles on strategy and managing the multinational in *Academy of Management Journal, Management Science, Organization Science, Strategic Management Journal, Journal of International Business Studies, Sloan Management Review, Harvard Business Review,* and others. Mr. Kim's current research focuses on strategy and management in the knowledge economy.

CONSTANTINOS C. MARKIDES is an associate professor of strategic and international management and the past director of the Accelerated Development Program at London Business School. His publications have appeared in journals such as *Harvard Business Review, Sloan Management Review, Directors & Boards, Long Range Planning, British Journal of Management, Journal of International Business Studies,* and *Strategic Management Journal.* He is the author of *Diversification Refocusing and Economic Performance* (MIT Press, 1995) and *Crafting Strategy: A Journey into the Mind of the Strategist* (Harvard Business School Press, 1998). He is also an associate editor of *European Management Journal* and is on the editorial boards of *Strategic Management Journal* and *Academy of Management Journal.*

RENÉE MAUBORGNE is distinguished fellow and affiliate professor of Strategy and Management at INSEAD. She is also president of ITM Research, a research group committed to discovering ideas that matter in the knowledge economy. She has published a number of articles on strategy and managing the multinational in *Academy of Management Journal, Management Science, Organization Science, Strategic Management Journal, Journal of International Business Studies, Sloan Management Review, Harvard Business Review,* and others. Ms. Mauborgne's current research focuses on strategy and management in the knowledge economy.

JAMES A. NARUS is an associate professor at the Babcock Graduate School of Management, Wake Forest University. He specializes in issues relating to business market management and distribution channels. His current research and teaching interests include value assessment and value-based marketing, the management of firm's market offerings, and adaptive channels. Dr. Narus has written numerous articles on these topics in such journals as *Harvard Business Review, California*

Management Review, Sloan Management Review, and *Journal of Marketing.* He is the co-author, with Professor James C. Anderson, of *Business Market Management: Understanding, Creating, and Delivering Value* (Prentice-Hall, 1998).

DAVID K. PECAUT manages The Boston Consulting Group's Canadian operations, which as of 1993 also incorporate the practice of The Canada Consulting Group. His practice is wide-ranging but focuses heavily on issues of globalization, building brands, pricing, and competitive strategy. Mr. Pecaut's clients include major multinationals worldwide and span diverse sectors, including home appliances, consumer goods and retailing, packaging, and financial services. He has also built an international practice as an adviser on economic and industrial policy to governments in the Americas, Asia, and Europe. Prior to his career in consulting, Mr. Pecaut served as the president's adviser on strategic issues at a *Fortune* 1000 chemical company.

JEFFREY F. RAYPORT is an associate professor of business administration in the Service Management Unit at the Harvard Business School. His research is on the impact of new information technologies on service management and marketing strategies for business, with a focus on digital commerce in information-based and knowledge-intensive industries. As a consultant, Dr. Rayport has worked with corporations and professional practices in North and South America, Europe, Japan, and the Pacific Rim. His consulting work helps companies develop breakthrough service strategies in network-based or digital sectors of the economy.

GEORGE STALK, JR., is a senior vice president of The Boston Consulting Group and focuses his professional practice on international and time-based competition. He speaks regularly to business and industry associations on time-based competition and other topics. Based in Toronto, he has served as a consultant to a variety of leading manufacturing, retailing, and technology- and consumer-oriented companies. Mr. Stalk is the co-author of the critically acclaimed *Competing Across Time* and *Kaisha: The Japanese Corporation*; his articles have appeared in numerous business publications.

JOHN J. SVIOKLA is an associate professor in the Management Information Systems Area at the Harvard Business School. Professor Sviokla's current work focuses on electronic commerce and knowledge management, in particular, how managers can use the power of technology to create value for customers and extract value through superior financial performance. With Professor Jeffrey F. Rayport, he has collaborated on "The New Locus of Value Creation," in *Intelligent Environments;* "Managing in the Marketspace" and "Exploiting the Virtual Value Chain" in *Harvard Business Review;* and a recent videotape on marketspace concepts. With another colleague, Professor Benson Shapiro, Sviokla has edited *Seeking Customers* and *Keeping Customers* (Harvard Business School Press, 1993). Professor Sviokla is on the editorial board of *Journal of Electronic Commerce* and is an associate editor of *Organization Science.*

Index

Knowledge is Power.
(So don't forget to recharge.)

For e-mail updates on powerful new business ideas
and management issues, sign up for the *Harvard Business
Review* listserv at **www.hbsp.harvard.edu**.

For ideas any time keep the Harvard Business School
Publishing Web page in mind.

○ Access more than 7,500 articles, books, case studies, videos
  and CD-ROMs by leaders in management practice.
○ Search by author, key word, and more.
○ Order on-line and download *Harvard Business Review*
  articles any time.

Visit **www.hbsp.harvard.edu**, or call **(800) 668-6780**
or **(617) 496-1449**.

 Harvard Business School Publishing
The power of ideas at work.